Contents

You can hardly walk a block in any city centre without passing a sushi shop or noodle bar, but while sushi and soba noodles may be the most famous dishes of Japanese cuisine, there are many other wonderful and exciting dishes. Not only is Japanese food delicious but it is also low in fat, deceptively simple to prepare and beautiful in its presentation.

The traditional Japanese diet is undoubtedly one of the healthiest in the world. It uses the freshest of seasonal ingredients, has very little added fat and makes use of subtle seasonings to enhance the natural flavour of the food. Perhaps it is for these reasons that Japanese have the highest life expectancy in the world.

Japanese cooking places much emphasis on the freshness and quality of the produce, the careful preparation of the food and the presentation at the table. Japanese believe that food should look as good as it tastes, so garnishes are often used and the presentation is always beautiful.

The main ingredients in Japanese cuisine are rice, fresh fish and meat, soy bean products, including tofu, miso and soy sauce, noodles and a variety of fresh vegetables. Thankfully these ingredients are now familiar to many people outside of Japan and are widely available in supermarkets. Traditionally, green tea is served at the beginning of, throughout and at the end of every meal. Dishes are usually served all at once rather than in courses, and small portions are taken from each dish. Rice and miso soup are also usually served in abundance with every meal, including breakfast, alongside several side dishes.

Japanese essentials

BONITO FLAKES (katsuobushi)
Dried, smoked and cured bonito (a type of tuna) is shaved into flakes and sold as large or fine flakes. Large flakes are used to make dashi, while fine flakes are used as a garnish. It has a strong aroma but a smoky, mellow flavour. Store in airtight container.

BREADCRUMBS, JAPANESE (panko)
Available in two kinds (large and fine), they are larger than traditional breadcrumbs and make a very crisp coating for deep-fried food.

DAIKON, Fresh (takuan)
Pickled (oshinko)
A giant white radish resembling a large carrot. Raw, it has a fresh and mild flavour; cooked, it becomes sweet. It is often used in salads, as a garnish or grated into dipping sauces. Store wrapped in plastic in refrigerator.
When pickled in rice bran and salt, it is bright yellow, crunchy and very pungent. It's great to cleanse the palate between bites of food.

GREEN TEA POWDER (matcha)
A fine powder made by grinding high-grade green tea. Matcha is the tea used in the traditional Japanese tea ceremony and is also used to colour and flavour foods such as noodles, ice-cream and confectionery. It is available from Asian food stores.

MISO
Fermented soybean paste available in different grades, colour and strengths. Generally the darker the miso, the saltier the taste and denser the texture. Two types are mainly used: white (shiro) which has a sweet mild flavour and is a gold colour; and red (aka) which is more earthy and salty, and is a dark caramel colour. Store airtight for up to one year in refrigerator.

PEPPER, JAPANESE
(sansho)
Ground seeds of the Japanese prickly ash. It has a spicy aroma and flavour and has a slightly numbing quality like Sichuan pepper which you can use if you cannot find Japanese pepper.

PICKLED GINGER
Pickled ginger can be either pink (gari) or red (beni-shoga) coloured and is available from Asian food shops. The pink variety are paper-thin shavings of ginger pickled in a mixture of vinegar, sugar and natural colouring. It is often used with sushi or rich food as a palate cleanser. The pickled red strips are used as filling in sushi rolls.

RED BEAN PASTE
(azuki bean paste)
Sweet paste made from slowly cooking small red beans (azuki) in a sugar syrup.

SEAWEED, Dried kelp (konbu)
Basis of dashi. Sold in wide strips, it often has a white powdery substance that coats the surface. Wipe with a damp cloth to discard any grit but do not wipe clean or rinse so as not to remove surface flavour. It develops a bitter flavour if overcooked so always remove just before water boils. To enhance flavour, cut along edges before adding to water.

SEAWEED, Nori
Nori is a dried laver seaweed which grows on rocks in bays and at the mouths of rivers. Crisp paper-like sheets of compressed seaweed, commonly used to wrap sushi. It is sometimes sold pre-toasted (yaki-nori), if not, place in large frying pan or under grill to toast quickly on one side until crisp. It also comes finely shredded or as flakes (ao-nori) for sprinkling as a garnish.

SEAWEED, Wakame
Wakame is a highly nutritious seaweed that is black when purchased dried, but reconstitutes to a bright-green colour. Soak for only 5 minutes or it will go mushy. The leaves are usually stripped from the central vein.

SESAME SEEDS
Small oval white or black seeds (goma) available raw, toasted or ground to a paste. Sesame oil is a strongly flavoured oil extracted from toasted seeds. A spicy version infused with chilli is popular for sprinkling over noodle soups.

SEVEN-SPICE MIX
(shichimi togarashi)
It always includes togarashi, a red hot Japanese chilli. The remaining six ingredients are flexible but often include mustard seeds, sesame seeds, poppy seeds, sansho pepper, shiso and nori flakes.

SOYA BEANS
Available dried as small yellowish oval beans that require soaking before use, precooked in cans, or fresh or frozen in the pod (edamame). Rich in protein and used to make tofu, miso and soy sauce.

TOFU
Also called bean curd, this creamy flavoured, high-protein food is made by setting the whitish liquid that results when soya beans and water are ground together. Available in a variety of textures: silken, a very soft, fragile tofu is used in dressings and desserts; silken firm is slightly firmer and used in soups and salads or is deep-fried; firm is a dense, textured tofu that holds together well for stews and stir-fries.

WASABI
Wasabi paste is a hot, very pungent mixture made from the knobbly green root of the Japanese wasabi plant (often referred to as japanese horseradish). Once opened, the paste must be refrigerated. Also available in powdered form to be mixed to a paste when needed.

Sesame salt (gomasio)

¼ cup (35g) white sesame seeds
1 teaspoon salt

1 Dry-fry seeds in medium frying pan until toasted; cool.
2 Blend, process or grind seeds and salt until coarse.

prep + cook time 20 minutes (+ cooling) **makes** ¼ cup
nutritional count per tablespoon 6.5g total fat (0.8g saturated fat);
297kJ (71 cal); 0.1g carbohydrate; 2.6g protein; 1.2g fibre
tips If using an electric blender, do not over process as you want a
grainy texture not a paste.
Gomasio is an excellent seasoning for rice, soups, stews and vegetables.

Red miso sauce

⅓ cup (80ml) water
¼ cup (75g) white miso
¼ cup (60ml) mirin
¼ cup (55g) caster (superfine) sugar
1½ tablespoons light soy sauce
1 tablespoon red miso

1 Stir ingredients in small saucepan over low heat until sugar dissolves; cool 5 minutes.

prep + cook time 10 minutes (+ cooling) **makes** ½ cup
nutritional count per tablespoon 1g total fat (0.1g saturated fat); 305kJ (73 cal); 13.1g carbohydrate; 2.2g protein; 0.9g fibre
tips Add some crushed dried chilli for extra flavour.
This sauce is typically served as an accompaniment to tofu and vegetables.

Pickled ginger

500g (1 pound) fresh ginger, peeled, sliced thinly
1 tablespoon salt
1½ cups (375ml) white vinegar
1 cup (220g) caster (superfine) sugar

1 Combine ginger and salt in medium bowl; stand 1 hour. Rinse ginger under cold running water; drain.
2 Stir vinegar and sugar in medium saucepan over heat, without boiling, until sugar dissolves. Bring to the boil. Add ginger; return to the boil.
3 Bottle in sterilised jars; seal.

prep + cook time 25 minutes (+ standing) **makes** 2 cups
nutritional count per tablespoon 0.1g total fat (0g saturated fat); 184kJ (44 cal); 10.2g carbohydrate; 0.2g protein; 0.6g fibre
tip To sterilise jars, place clean open jars and lids in preheated oven at 120°C/250°F for 15 minutes. Remove from oven when ready to fill.

Tempura dipping sauce

1¼ cups (310ml) primary dashi (see recipe page 116)
⅓ cup (80ml) japanese soy sauce
¼ cup (60ml) mirin

1 Bring ingredients to the boil in small saucepan.
2 Reduce heat to low; keep warm until ready to serve.

prep + cook time 10 minutes **makes** 2¾ cups
nutritional count per tablespoon 0g total fat (0g saturated fat);
13kJ (3 cal); 0.2g carbohydrate; 0.2g protein; 0g fibre

Starters

Deep-fried tofu in broth

300g (9½ ounces) firm tofu
2 tablespoons cornflour (cornstarch)
vegetable oil, for deep-frying
¾ cup (180ml) primary dashi (see recipe page 116)
2 tablespoons japanese soy sauce
2 tablespoons mirin
40g (1½ ounces) daikon, grated finely
4cm (1½-inch) piece fresh ginger (20g), grated
1 green onion (scallion), chopped finely
2 teaspoons smoked dried bonito flakes

1 Press tofu between two chopping boards with weight on top, raise
one end; stand 25 minutes.
2 Cut tofu into eight pieces; pat dry between layers of absorbent paper.
Toss tofu in cornflour; shake away excess. Heat oil in medium saucepan;
deep-fry tofu, in batches, until golden. Drain on absorbent paper.
3 Bring dashi, sauce and mirin to the boil in small saucepan.
4 Divide tofu among bowls; top with daikon, ginger and green onion.
Pour over dashi mixture; sprinkle with bonito flakes.

prep + cook time 30 minutes (+ standing) **serves** 4
nutritional count per serving 10.4g total fat (1.4g saturated fat);
723kJ (173 cal); 5.6g carbohydrate; 10.4g protein; 5.4g fibre

Grilled eggplant with miso

9 baby eggplants (540g)
2 teaspoons salt
2 tablespoons vegetable oil
2 tablespoons white miso
1 tablespoon white sugar
1 tablespoon sake
1 tablespoon mirin
1 egg yolk
1 teaspoon seven-spice mix
2 tablespoons white sesame seeds, toasted
4 green onions (scallions), chopped finely

1 Cut eggplant lengthways into 1cm (½-inch) thick slices. Place in colander, sprinkle with salt; stand 30 minutes.

2 Rinse eggplant; drain on absorbent paper. Brush eggplant with oil. Cook eggplant, in batches, on heated grill plate (or grill or barbecue) until soft.

3 Preheat grill.

4 Combine miso, sugar, sake, mirin and egg yolk in small bowl. Place eggplant, in single layer, on baking-paper-lined oven tray. Spread with miso mixture; sprinkle with spice mix. Grill eggplant until miso starts to bubble. Serve eggplant sprinkled with seeds and green onion.

prep + cook time 40 minutes (+ standing) **serves** 6
nutritional count per serving 9.8g total fat (1.3g saturated fat); 564kJ (135 cal); 7.1g carbohydrate; 3.2g protein; 2.9g fibre
tip Toast the sesame seeds in a deep frying pan over low heat for about 3 minutes, shaking the pan constantly, until the seeds begin to pop.

Crispy beef and potato patties

3 medium potatoes (600g), chopped coarsely
2 teaspoons soy bean oil
½ small brown onion (40g), chopped finely
50g (1½ ounces) minced (ground) beef
2 eggs
½ cup (75g) plain (all-purpose) flour
1 cup (60g) japanese breadcrumbs
vegetable oil, for deep-frying
¼ small wombok (napa cabbage) (175g), sliced finely
1 medium lemon (140g), cut into wedges

1 Boil, steam or microwave potato until tender; drain. Mash until smooth.
2 Heat soy bean oil in medium frying pan; cook onion and beef, stirring, until onion softens and beef changes colour. Cool 5 minutes.
3 Combine mashed potato, beef mixture and one egg in medium bowl; season to taste. Using floured hands, shape potato mixture into eight oval patties. Toss patties in flour; shake away excess. Dip patties, one at a time, in lightly beaten egg, then in breadcrumbs.
4 Heat vegetable oil in saucepan; deep-fry patties, in batches, until golden and hot. Drain on absorbent paper. Serve with wombok and lemon wedges.

prep + cook time 50 minutes **serves** 4
nutritional count per serving 19.2g total fat (3.3g saturated fat); 1731kJ (414 cal); 42.3g carbohydrate; 14.4g protein; 5.6g fibre
tips Instead of pure vegetable oil to deep-fry, you can blend it (50/50) with sesame oil.
Patties can be served with soy sauce or tomato ketchup.

Scallops with miso sauce

12 scallops (300g), roe removed
1 clove garlic, crushed
2 tablespoons plain (all-purpose) flour
1 tablespoon vegetable oil
2 tablespoons dry white wine
1 tablespoon white miso
1 tablespoon mirin
1 teaspoon japanese soy sauce
1 teaspoon caster (superfine) sugar
1 tablespoon water
2 tablespoons double cream
2 teaspoons wholegrain mustard
200g (6½ ounces) watercress, chopped coarsely

1 Combine scallops and garlic in small bowl. Toss in flour; shake away excess.
2 Heat oil in medium frying pan; cook scallops both sides until browned lightly. Remove from pan; cover to keep warm.
3 Add wine, miso, mirin, sauce, sugar and the water to same pan; bring to the boil. Remove pan from heat; stir in cream and mustard until combined.
4 Serve scallops with sauce and watercress.

prep + cook time 20 minutes **serves** 4
nutritional count per serving 15.4g total fat (4.5g saturated fat); 890kJ (213 cal); 8.8g carbohydrate; 7.1g protein; 2.9g fibre

Tuna tartare

200g (6½ ounces) piece sashimi tuna, chopped finely
4 fresh japanese mint (shiso) leaves, chopped finely
1 green onion (scallion), chopped finely
1 teaspoon finely chopped brown onion
½ clove garlic, chopped finely
½ teaspoon wasabi paste
5mm (¼-inch) piece fresh ginger (5g), grated
¼ teaspoon freshly ground black pepper
dressing
1 tablespoon primary dashi (see recipe page 116)
1 tablespoon light soy sauce
1 tablespoon olive oil
2 teaspoons rice vinegar

1 Combine ingredients for dressing in small bowl.
2 Divide tuna among three small bowls. Mix one portion with mint;
another with green onion; and third with brown onion and garlic.
Shape four balls out of each tuna mixture.
3 Top herb balls with wasabi; top green onion balls with ginger;
sprinkle onion and garlic balls with pepper. Serve balls with dressing.

prep time 20 minutes **makes** 12
nutritional count per ball 1.8g total fat (0.3g saturated fat); 150kJ (36 cal);
0.2g carbohydrate; 4.5g protein; 0g fibre
tip Use a combination of basil and mint leaves if you cannot find any
japanese mint.

Grilled squid

8 whole baby squid (400g)
¼ cup (60ml) japanese soy sauce
¼ cup (60ml) mirin
1 teaspoon caster (superfine) sugar
¼ teaspoon seven-spice mix

1 Gently pull head and entrails away from squid body; remove and discard quill. Cut tentacles from head, just below eyes; remove and discard beak. Gently pull away outer membrane from hood; wash hood and tentacles well.
2 Bring sauce, mirin and sugar to the boil in small saucepan. Reduce heat; simmer, uncovered, about 3 minutes or until sauce thickens slightly. Cool 5 minutes
3 Combine squid hoods and tentacles with soy mixture in medium bowl. Cover; refrigerate 30 minutes.
4 Cook squid mixture on heated oiled grill plate (or grill or barbecue) until tender. Slice hoods thinly; serve sprinkled with spice mix.

prep + cook time 30 minutes (+ cooling & refrigeration) **serves** 4
nutritional count per serving 2.7g total fat (0.6g saturated fat); 460kJ (110 cal); 3.3g carbohydrate; 17.7g protein; 0.1g fibre

Deep-fried prawns with dipping sauce

20 uncooked large king prawns
  (shrimp) (1.4kg)
¼ cup (35g) plain (all-purpose)
  flour
¼ teaspoon salt
¼ teaspoon white pepper
1 egg
2 teaspoons water
1 cup (60g) japanese
  breadcrumbs
¼ cup (60ml) sesame oil
vegetable oil, for deep-frying
1 medium lemon (140g),
  cut into wedges

dipping sauce
⅔ cup (170g) mayonnaise
1½ tablespoons japanese pickled
  cucumber, chopped finely
1 tablespoon rice vinegar
1 spring onion, white part only,
  chopped finely
2 tablespoons finely chopped
  fresh flat-leaf parsley
1 clove garlic, crushed

1 Make dipping sauce.
2 Shell and devein prawns, leaving tails intact.
3 Combine flour, salt and pepper in shallow bowl. Lightly beat egg with
the water in small bowl. Working with one prawn at a time, hold it by the
tail (being careful not to coat the tail) and lightly coat with seasoned flour;
shake away excess. Dip prawn in egg mixture, then in breadcrumbs.
4 Place sesame oil in medium saucepan; top up with enough vegetable
oil to deep-fry. Heat oils; deep-fry prawns, in batches, until golden. Drain
on absorbent paper. Serve with dipping sauce and lemon wedges.
dipping sauce Combine ingredients in small bowl. Refrigerate until
ready to serve.

prep + cook time 30 minutes **serves** 4
nutritional count per serving 43.7g total fat (5.9g saturated fat);
2789kJ (667 cal); 26g carbohydrate; 41.4g protein; 2.1g fibre
tips To prevent prawns curling up too much during cooking, before coating,
make three cuts along belly of each prawn. Turn prawns over and press
down gently along the length of the body to flatten slightly.
Use dill pickles if you can't find japanese pickled cucumber.

Crispy prawns and noodles

12 uncooked large king prawns (shrimp) (840g)
180g (5½ ounces) dried somen noodles
1 cup (150g) plain (all-purpose) flour
1 egg yolk
1 cup (250ml) iced water
½ sheet toasted seaweed (yaki-nori), cut into 12 long strips
vegetable oil, for deep-frying
soy and ginger dipping sauce
½ cup (125ml) japanese soy sauce
2cm (¾-inch) piece fresh ginger (10g), grated
1 teaspoon caster (superfine) sugar

1 Combine ingredients for soy and ginger dipping sauce in small bowl. Refrigerate until required.
2 Shell and devein prawns, leaving tails intact. Break noodles into same lengths as prawns, not including tail; place on board.
3 Whisk flour, egg yolk and the water in small bowl until just combined. Dip prawns into batter; roll prawns, one at a time, over noodles to coat.
4 Wrap a seaweed strip around centre of each noodle-coated prawn, dampen ends with a little water and press to seal.
5 Heat oil in saucepan; deep-fry prawns, in batches, until golden and cooked. Drain on absorbent paper. Serve prawns with dipping sauce.

prep + cook time 40 minutes **serves** 4
nutritional count per serving 16.7g total fat (2.4g saturated fat); 2224kJ (532 cal); 59.6g carbohydrate; 33.1g protein; 3g fibre
tip To prevent prawns curling up too much during cooking, before coating, make three cuts along belly of each prawns. Turn prawns over and press down gently along the length of the body to flatten slightly.

Chilled tofu with ginger and green onion

600g (1¼ pounds) silken firm tofu
4cm (1½-inch) piece fresh ginger (20g), grated
2 green onions (scallions), chopped finely
2 teaspoons black sesame seeds, toasted
2 japanese mint (shiso) leaves, shredded finely
1 teaspoon bonito flakes
1 tablespoon japanese soy sauce
2 teaspoons chilli sesame oil

1 Press tofu between two chopping boards with weight on top,
raise one end; stand 25 minutes.
2 Halve each block of tofu; divide among plates. Top with ginger,
green onion, seeds, mint and bonito flakes.
3 Serve drizzled with sauce and sesame oil.

prep time 10 minutes (+ standing) **serves** 4
nutritional count per serving 14.1g total fat (1.9g saturated fat);
928kJ (222 cal); 0.2g carbohydrate; 18.8g protein; 10.7g fibre
tips Be careful when working with silken tofu as it is very soft and
breaks easily.
Use a mix of basil and mint leaves if you cannot find japanese mint.

Seafood and vegetable fritters

8 uncooked large king prawns (shrimp) (560g)
8 scallops (200g), without roe
1 medium carrot (120g)
200g (6½ ounces) daikon
1 medium brown onion (150g), sliced thinly
180g (5½ ounces) green beans, sliced finely
⅓ cup coarsely chopped fresh japanese parsley (mitsuba)
¼ cup (35g) plain (all-purpose) flour
1 quantity tempura batter (see recipe page 332)
vegetable oil, for deep-frying
½ cup (125ml) sesame oil
1 cup (250ml) tempura dipping sauce (see recipe page 15)

1 Shell and devein prawns; chop prawns and scallops coarsely.
2 Cut carrot and daikon into thin strips.
3 Combine seafood, vegetables, mitsuba and flour in large bowl.
Place tempura batter in another large bowl; lightly fold seafood
mixture through batter.
4 Heat combined oils in large saucepan; deep-fry tablespoons
of seafood mixture, in batches, until golden and cooked through.
Drain on absorbent paper.
5 Serve fritters with dipping sauce.

prep + cook time 45 minutes **makes** 48
nutritional count per fritter 1.9g total fat (0.2g saturated fat);
209kJ (50 cal); 5.9g carbohydrate; 2.1g protein; 0.4g fibre
tips Ready-made tempura dipping sauce is available from most
Asian grocers.
Flat-leaf parsley can be substituted for mitsuba if you cannot find it.

Salmon and tofu balls

200g (6½ ounces) silken tofu
400g (12½ ounces) can red salmon, drained
2 spring onions, chopped finely
2cm (¾-inch) piece fresh ginger (10g), grated
1 clove garlic, crushed
2 tablespoons plain (all-purpose) flour
1 tablespoon japanese soy sauce
2 teaspoons mirin
1 egg
vegetable oil, for deep-frying
wasabi mayonnaise dipping sauce
1 teaspoon japanese soy sauce
1 teaspoon mirin
1 teaspoon rice vinegar
½ teaspoon wasabi paste
½ cup (150g) mayonnaise

1 Make wasabi mayonnaise dipping sauce. Refrigerate until required.
2 Press tofu between two chopping boards with weight on top, raise
one end; stand 25 minutes.
3 Discard skin and bones from salmon; coarsely mash in medium bowl.
Stir in tofu, onion, ginger, garlic, flour, sauce, mirin and egg until combined.
4 Heat oil in large saucepan; deep-fry tablespoons of salmon mixture,
in batches, until golden. Drain on absorbent paper.
5 Serve with dipping sauce and lemon wedges, if you like.
wasabi mayonnaise dipping sauce Whisk sauce, mirin, vinegar and
wasabi in small bowl until smooth; whisk in mayonnaise.

prep + cook time 30 minutes (+ standing) **makes** 25
nutritional count per ball 5.1g total fat (0.8g saturated fat);
305kJ (73 cal); 2g carbohydrate; 4.4g protein; 0.8g fibre

Oyster platter

24 fresh oysters (600g), chilled
2 teaspoons finely grated lime rind
2 tablespoons salmon roe
2 teaspoons white sesame seeds,
   toasted

ponzu dressing
5 x 2cm (¾-inch) pieces kelp
   (konbu)
1½ tablespoons japanese
   soy sauce
1½ tablespoons sake
2 teaspoons lemon juice
2 teaspoons lime juice
2 teaspoons mirin
2 teaspoons rice vinegar
2 teaspoons bonito flakes
½ teaspoon caster (superfine)
   sugar

wasabi dressing
¼ cup (60ml) rice vinegar
1 tablespoon pouring cream
2 teaspoons wasabi paste
2 teaspoons mirin
½ teaspoon caster (superfine)
   sugar

ginger and sesame dressing
1½ tablespoons rice vinegar
1½ tablespoons sake
1 tablespoon japanese soy sauce
1cm (½-inch) piece fresh
   ginger (5g), grated
1 teaspoon caster (superfine)
   sugar
½ teaspoon sesame oil

1 Make ponzu dressing, wasabi dressing and ginger and sesame dressing.
2 Arrange oysters on platter. Drizzle eight oysters with ponzu dressing;
sprinkle with rind. Drizzle eight oysters with wasabi dressing; top with roe.
Drizzle remaining oysters with ginger and sesame dressing; sprinkle
with seeds.

ponzu dressing Wipe kelp with damp cloth; cut into strips. Combine
kelp with remaining ingredients in small bowl. Cover; refrigerate 24 hours.
Strain through muslin or fine sieve into small bowl.

wasabi dressing Whisk ingredients in small bowl until smooth.
Cover; refrigerate 30 minutes.

ginger and sesame dressing Combine ingredients in small bowl.
Cover; refrigerate 30 minutes.

prep time 15 minutes (+ refrigeration) **makes** 24
nutritional count per oyster 1g total fat (0.4g saturated fat);
92kJ (22 cal); 0.6g carbohydrate; 1.8g protein; 0g fibre
tip Each dressing makes ⅓ cup (80ml) and is enough to dress 24 oysters.

Nori, sesame and parmesan pastries

2 sheets toasted seaweed (nori), shredded
½ cup (40g) finely grated parmesan cheese
2 tablespoons white sesame seeds, toasted
½ teaspoon caster (superfine) sugar
½ teaspoon sea salt flakes
1 pinch ground black pepper
2 sheets frozen puff pastry, thawed
30g (1 ounce) butter, melted

1 Preheat oven to 220°C/425°F.
2 Combine seaweed, cheese, seeds, sugar, salt and pepper in
medium bowl.
3 Place pastry sheets on two pieces of baking paper. Brush pastry with
butter. Sprinkle pastry with two-thirds of the cheese mixture, pressing
mixture down into pastry. Using baking paper, fold each pastry sheet
in half; press down to seal. Brush pastry with remaining butter; sprinkle
with remaining cheese mixture, pressing mixture down into pastry.
Fold sheets in half lengthways to form rectangle; press down to seal.
4 Place pastry on baking-paper-lined oven tray; refrigerate 30 minutes.
5 Using a sharp knife, trim ends; cut pastry into 1cm (½-inch) slices.
Place slices, cut-side down, about 3cm (1¼ inches) apart on tray.
6 Bake pastries about 15 minutes or until puffed and golden.

prep + cook time 1 hour (+ refrigeration) **makes** about 32
nutritional count per pastry 3.9g total fat (1g saturated fat);
234kJ (56 cal); 3.8g carbohydrate; 1.2g protein; 0.2g fibre
tip Use scissors to finely shred the sheets of seaweed.

Miso garlic dip with cucumber

1 pinch dashi granules
1½ tablespoons hot water
2 tablespoons white miso
1 tablespoon red miso
1 tablespoon sake
2 teaspoons caster (superfine) sugar
2 teaspoons mirin
½ teaspoon sesame oil
2 cloves garlic, crushed
4 lebanese cucumbers (520g)

1 Whisk dashi and the water in small bowl until dissolved; whisk in miso, sake, sugar, mirin, oil and garlic. Season with pepper. Refrigerate 1 hour.
2 Halve cucumbers lengthways; discard seeds with teaspoon. Cut cucumber into batons.
3 Serve dip with cucumber.

prep time 15 minutes (+ refrigeration) **serves** 4
nutritional count per serving 1.8g total fat (0.2g saturated fat); 293kJ (70 cal); 9g carbohydrate; 2.8g protein; 2.8g fibre
tips You can use other vegetables as accompaniments, such as carrots, asparagus spears or snow peas.
You can also add ¼ cup finely chopped roasted peanuts to the dip for extra crunch.

Wasabi salmon

650g (1¼ pounds) salmon fillet, skinned, cut into cubes
2 teaspoons wasabi paste
¼ cup (60ml) japanese soy sauce
½ teaspoon sesame oil
cucumber dipping sauce
½ lebanese cucumber (65g)
⅓ cup (80ml) rice wine vinegar
1 tablespoon sugar

1 Combine salmon, wasabi, sauce and oil in medium bowl;
stand 15 minutes.
2 Meanwhile, make cucumber dipping sauce.
3 Drain salmon; discard marinade. Heat large oiled frying pan;
cook salmon, in batches, over high heat about 20 seconds each side.
Serve salmon with dipping sauce.
cucumber dipping sauce Halve cucumber lengthways; discard
seeds with a teaspoon. Chop cucumber finely. Place in small bowl with
remaining ingredients; stir until sugar dissolves.

prep + cook time 35 minutes (+ standing) **makes** 48
nutritional count per piece 1g total fat (0.2g saturated fat); 92kJ (22 cal);
0.4g carbohydrate; 2.7g protein; 0g fibre
tip A non-stick pan is best to use for cooking the salmon. Don't overcook
the salmon, it should be served rare.

Beef salad

1 tablespoon vegetable oil
2 beef fillet steaks (500g)
100g (3 ounces) baby rocket leaves
1 green onion (scallion), sliced thinly
mustard and soy dressing
2 tablespoons japanese soy sauce
1 tablespoon rice vinegar
1 tablespoon sake
1 tablespoon olive oil
1 teaspoon caster (superfine) sugar
½ teaspoon japanese mustard
½ teaspoon sesame oil
2cm (¾-inch) piece fresh ginger (10g), grated
1 clove garlic, crushed

1 Heat oil in heavy-based frying pan; cook steak until well browned. Plunge steak into bowl of iced-water; remove steak, pat dry with absorbent paper.
2 Make mustard and soy dressing.
3 Slice beef thinly; arrange on plates. Top with rocket; drizzle over dressing. Sprinkle with green onion.
mustard and soy dressing Combine ingredients in small bowl.

prep + cook time 20 minutes **serves** 4
nutritional count per serving 15.9g total fat (3.9g saturated fat); 1116kJ (267 cal); 2g carbohydrate; 27.4g protein; 0.5g fibre
tip To make this recipe a light main course for two, serve it with steamed rice or noodles.

49

Spicy tofu fries

1kg (2 pounds) firm tofu
¼ cup (60ml) japanese soy sauce
2 tablespoons white miso
2 teaspoons chilli sesame oil
4cm (1½-inch) piece fresh ginger (20g), grated
4 cloves garlic, crushed
½ cup (65g) potato starch
1 tablespoon seven-spice mix
vegetable oil, for deep-frying

1 Press tofu between two chopping boards with weight on top,
raise one end; stand 2 hours.
2 Cut tofu into 1.5cm (¾-inch) thick slices, then cut slices into
2cm x 6cm (¾-inch x 2½ inches) long fingers.
3 Combine sauce, miso, sesame oil, ginger and garlic in a jug.
Pour half the marinade into shallow, non-metallic dish; add tofu.
Pour over remaining marinade, gently shaking dish to help coat tofu.
Cover; refrigerate overnight.
4 Combine potato starch and spice mix in shallow bowl; season.
Scrape any excess marinade from tofu; dip tofu into seasoned starch,
shake off excess.
5 Heat oil in saucepan; deep-fry tofu, in batches, until golden. Drain
on absorbent paper. Season with salt.

prep + cook time 2 hours 30 minutes (+ standing & refrigeration)
serves 8
nutritional count per serving 18g total fat (2.4g saturated fat);
1150kJ (275 cal); 7.7g carbohydrate; 16.2g protein; 9.8g fibre
tips Potato starch is similar to cornflour but stronger, so use a little more
cornflour if you cannot find any potato starch.
Serve this starter with tempura dipping sauce (see recipe page 15).

Cabbage rolls

3 dried shiitake mushrooms
1 teaspoon sesame oil
¼ cup (60ml) vegetable oil
5 green onions (scallions), sliced
2cm (¾-inch) piece fresh
    ginger (10g), grated
2 cloves garlic, crushed
½ teaspoon japanese pepper
400g (12½ ounces) minced
    (ground) pork
½ cup (100g) japanese rice
    (koshihikari)
⅓ cup finely chopped japanese
    parsley (mitsuba)

1 large wombok (napa cabbage)
    (1.3kg)
¼ cup (60ml) rice vinegar
2 tablespoons japanese soy sauce
2 tablespoons sake
2 tablespoons mirin
1 teaspoon dashi granules
dipping sauce
½ teaspoon sesame oil
2 teaspoons mirin
2 teaspoons caster (superfine)
    sugar
1½ tablespoons rice vinegar
¼ cup (60ml) japanese soy sauce

1 Place mushrooms in small heatproof bowl, cover with boiling water, stand 20 minutes; drain. Discard stems; chop caps finely.
2 Meanwhile, heat sesame oil and 1 tablespoon of the vegetable oil in small frying pan; cook onion, ginger, garlic and pepper, stirring, 2 minutes or until onion has softened. Cool.
3 Combine pork, mushrooms, rice, mitsuba and onion mixture in large bowl.
4 Bring a large saucepan of water to the boil. Trim 5cm (2 inches) from white base of wombok; discard base. Place remaining wombok in boiling water; simmer, uncovered, 5 minutes, or until leaves have wilted. Drain leaves over large bowl; reserve 3 cups (750ml) cooking liquid. While liquid is hot, add vinegar, soy, sake, mirin, dashi and remaining vegetable oil.
5 Lay 16 of the largest leaves, vein-side down, on work bench. Spoon rice mixture onto base of each leaf. Roll up, tucking in sides to enclose filling.
6 Line a large saucepan with three quarters of the remaining wombok leaves; place rolls on top, seam-side down. Cover with remaining leaves; pour over reserved cooking liquid. Bring to the boil. Reduce heat; simmer, covered, about 1 hour or until pork and rice are cooked through.
7 Make dipping sauce. Serve cabbage rolls with dipping sauce.
dipping sauce Combine ingredients in small bowl.

prep + cook time 1 hour 50 minutes (+ standing) **makes** 16
nutritional count per roll 5.8g total fat (1.2g saturated fat); 510kJ (122 cal); 8g carbohydrate; 7.1g protein; 3.1g fibre

Daikon hash browns

1 medium daikon (600g), peeled, cut into large chunks
1 small brown onion (80g), chopped finely
2cm (¾-inch) piece fresh ginger (10g), grated
1½ tablespoons coarsely chopped fresh flat-leaf parsley
1 egg
⅓ cup (60g) potato starch
¼ cup (30g) plain (all-purpose) flour
1½ teaspoons salt
vegetable oil, for shallow-frying

1 Place daikon in large saucepan covered with cold water; bring to
the boil. Cook, uncovered, about 25 minutes or until tender; drain.
Cool 10 minutes.
2 Coarsely grate daikon into medium bowl lined with clean tea towel.
Gather tea towel up to enclose daikon; squeeze out excess moisture.
Place daikon in another medium bowl with onion, ginger, parsley and egg.
Stir in potato starch, flour and salt; season with white pepper.
3 Fill a deep frying pan with enough vegetable oil to come 5mm (¼ inch)
up side; heat. Working in batches, drop tablespoons of mixture into oil;
flatten mixture with back of a spoon. Cook about 2 minutes each side or
until crisp and golden. Drain on absorbent paper.

prep + cook time 1 hour **makes** 12
nutritional count per hash brown 7.3g total fat (1g saturated fat);
426kJ (102 cal); 7.1g carbohydrate; 1.3g protein; 1.3g fibre
tips Potato starch is similar to cornflour but stronger, so use a little more
cornflour if you cannot find any potato starch.
Serve this starter with tempura dipping sauce (see recipe page 15).

Grilled tofu with sesame and spinach miso

600g (1¼ pounds) firm tofu
¼ cup (75g) white miso
1 teaspoon sugar
1 tablespoon mirin
2 tablespoons primary dashi (see recipe page 116)
1 tablespoon tahini
8 spinach leaves
1 tablespoon finely shredded lemon rind

1 Press tofu between two chopping boards with weight on top, raise one end; stand 25 minutes.
2 Stir miso, sugar, mirin and dashi in small saucepan over heat, without boiling, until sugar dissolves. Stir in tahini.
3 Boil, steam or microwave spinach until just wilted. Squeeze out excess liquid. Blend or process spinach with half the miso mixture.
4 Preheat grill.
5 Cut tofu in half crossways through the block, then into 3cm (1¼-inch) slices; pat dry with absorbent paper. Place slices on oiled oven tray; grill about 3 minutes or until browned lightly. Spread half the tofu pieces with miso mixture, then spread remaining tofu with spinach miso mixture. Place under grill a further 2 minutes or until miso is browned lightly. Serve sprinkled with rind.

prep + cook time 20 minutes (+ standing) **serves** 4
nutritional count per serving 19.4g total fat (2.6g saturated fat); 1450kJ (347 cal); 11.4g carbohydrate; 25.4g protein; 15.1g fibre
tip Use a lemon zester to make lemon rind strips for decoration; soak them in iced water to make them curl.

Steamed custard

4 uncooked medium king prawns (shrimp) (180g)
75g (2½ ounces) chicken breast fillet, sliced thinly
3 teaspoons japanese soy sauce
1 teaspoon sake
1¾ cups (430ml) primary dashi (see recipe page 116)
1 tablespoon sake, extra
4 eggs
4 fresh shiitake mushrooms, stems removed, quartered
½ small carrot (35g), halved lengthways, sliced thinly
8 spinach leaves, blanched, chopped coarsely
1 tablespoon finely shredded lemon rind

1 Shell and devein prawns, leaving tails intact.
2 Combine chicken with 1 teaspoon of the sauce and sake in medium bowl; stand 10 minutes.
3 Combine dashi, remaining sauce and extra sake in medium bowl; whisk in egg. Strain egg mixture through fine or cloth-lined sieve into large jug.
4 Divide chicken, prawns and vegetables among four ¾-cup (180ml) tea or coffee cups; pour egg mixture over chicken mixture until 1cm (½ inch) from top of the cup. Cover each cup with plastic wrap.
5 Place cups in steamer, allowing space between cups for the steam to circulate, cover. Steam over large saucepan of boiling water about 20 minutes or until just set. Remove plastic wrap; place hot cups on saucers or small plates. Serve sprinkled with rind.

prep + cook time 35 minutes (+ standing) **serves** 4
nutritional count per serving 7.5g total fat (2.3g saturated fat); 648kJ (155 cal); 1.7g carbohydrate; 18.6g protein; 1.2g fibre
tips Individual soufflé dishes or ramekins can be used if you don't have small tea or coffee cups.
To blanch spinach, place leaves in a medium heatproof bowl, cover with boiling water, stand 1 minute; drain, squeezing spinach to remove excess moisture.
Use a lemon zester to make lemon rind strips for decoration; soak them in iced water to make them curl.

Thick omelette

8 eggs, beaten lightly
1 tablespoon water or dashi
2 teaspoons sugar
3 teaspoons mirin
2 teaspoons light soy sauce
2 tablespoons vegetable oil
⅓ cup (80ml) japanese soy sauce
60g (2 ounces) daikon, grated finely

1 Stir egg, the water, sugar, mirin and light soy in large jug until
sugar dissolves.
2 Heat a little of the oil in a traditional square frying pan or medium
(20cm/8-inch) frying pan over medium heat. Pour in enough egg mixture
to just cover base of pan; cook, tilting pan to spread mixture evenly.
Break any large air bubbles so omelette lies flat. When mixture
is almost set, run spatula around edge of pan to loosen omelette.
3 Starting from back of pan, fold omelette into three towards front of
pan. Gently push folded omelette to back of pan.
4 Lightly oil pan again, repeat process, lifting up the cooked omelette
so egg mixture runs underneath it. When nearly cooked, fold in three,
starting with the omelette already cooked and folded. Repeat this step
until all mixture is used.
5 Tip omelette onto bamboo mat and wrap firmly to form a compact
rectangle. Cool omelette; cut into 1cm (½-inch) slices. Serve with
japanese soy and daikon.

prep + cook time 15 minutes (+ cooling) **serves** 4
nutritional count per serving 21.2g total fat (4.8g saturated fat);
1133kJ (271 cal); 3.6g carbohydrate; 16.5g protein; 0.2g fibre
tips Sliced omelette can also be used for sushi or cut lengthways into
long, thin strips and used as a filling for sushi rolls.
To give the omelette a colourful centre, wrap the first omelette around
cooked carrot and green onion. Or add a toasted nori sheet between
each layer of egg.

Savoury pancake

2 cups (300g) plain (all-purpose) flour
1½ teaspoons baking powder
1½ cups (375ml) primary dashi (see recipe page 116)
1 egg, beaten lightly
2 large cabbage leaves
125g (4 ounces) minced (ground) pork
2 tablespoons vegetable oil
½ cup (125ml) japanese worcestershire sauce
2 tablespoons (46g) drained red pickled ginger
1 tablespoon shredded seaweed (ao-nori)
¼ cup (3g) smoked dried bonito flakes

1 Sift flour and baking powder into medium bowl. Gradually stir in combined dashi and egg, mixing quickly until smooth; do not overmix. Cover; stand 30 minutes.
2 Discard thick ribs from cabbage leaves; slice leaves thinly. Add cabbage and pork to batter, season with pepper; mix gently.
3 Heat a quarter of the oil in medium frying pan over low heat. Add a quarter of the batter, flatten with spatula. When bubbles begin to appear, turn over and brush cooked side with sauce. Turn pancake over again and brush other side with sauce. Quickly repeat once more, so sauce caramelises. Remove from pan, cover; keep warm. Repeat with remaining oil and batter to make four pancakes in total.
4 Serve pancakes sprinkled with pickled ginger, seaweed and bonito flakes.

prep + cook time 20 minutes (+ standing) **serves** 4
nutritional count per serving 14.2g total fat (2.7g saturated fat); 1956kJ (468 cal); 64.3g carbohydrate; 18.6g protein; 4g fibre
tips Japanese worcestershire sauce comes in different strengths; most are milder than western worcestershire so adjust the amount added according to taste. Commercial or homemade tonkatsu sauce (see recipe page 291) makes a good substitute.

Fried tofu with daikon and ginger

600g (1 ¼ pounds) firm tofu
⅓ cup (50g) plain (all-purpose) flour
2 eggs, beaten lightly
⅓ cup (50g) black sesame seeds
⅓ cup (50g) white sesame seeds
vegetable oil, for deep-frying
120g (4 ounces) daikon, grated finely
2cm (¾ inch) piece fresh ginger (10g), grated
sauce
⅓ cup (80ml) primary dashi (see recipe page 116)
1 teaspoon mirin
1 tablespoon japanese soy sauce

1 Press tofu between two chopping boards with weight on top, raise one end; stand 25 minutes.
2 Cut tofu into 2.5cm (1-inch) cubes; toss in flour, shake off excess. Dip tofu in egg, then in combined seeds to coat.
3 Heat oil in medium saucepan; deep-fry tofu, in batches, until browned lightly all over. Drain on absorbent paper.
4 Meanwhile, make sauce.
5 Serve tofu with warm sauce and topped with daikon and ginger.
sauce Stir ingredients in small saucepan until heated through.

prep + cook time 20 minutes (+ standing) **serves** 4
nutritional count per serving 40.3g total fat (5.7g saturated fat); 2278kJ (545 cal); 10.4g carbohydrate; 29.4g protein; 14g fibre
tip If you like, you can add dried smoked bonito flakes to the sesame seeds or try coating the tofu with japanese breadcrumbs instead.

Gyozas (pot stickers)

325g (10½ ounces) cabbage, chopped finely
300g (9½ ounces) minced (ground) pork
4 green onions (scallions), chopped finely
1 egg, beaten lightly
2 tablespoons japanese soy sauce
1 tablespoon sake
2 teaspoons sesame oil
1 teaspoon sugar
¼ teaspoon white pepper
50 gyoza wrappers
1 tablespoon vegetable oil

1 Combine cabbage, pork, onion, egg, sauce, sake, sesame oil, sugar and pepper in medium bowl. Cover; refrigerate 1 hour.
2 Place one heaped teaspoon of pork mixture in centre of one wrapper; wet edge around one half of wrapper. Pleat to seal. Repeat with remaining pork mixture and wrappers.
3 Cover base of large frying pan with water; bring to the boil then add gyoza, in batches. Reduce heat; simmer, covered, 3 minutes.
4 Heat vegetable oil in same cleaned pan; cook gyoza, one side only, uncovered, in batches, until browned and slightly crisp. Drain on absorbent paper.

prep + cook time 30 minutes (+ refrigeration) **makes** 50
nutritional count per gyoza 1.2g total fat (0.3g saturated fat); 142kJ (34 cal); 3.4g carbohydrate; 2.1g protein; 0.4g fibre
tips You can vary the filling of these dumplings by adding chopped prawns (shrimp), cheese, capsicum or scrambled egg.
Serve with soy sauce mixed with chilli oil, or rice vinegar or ponzu sauce (see recipe page 273).

Spicy teriyaki tuna

¾ cup (180ml) japanese soy sauce
¼ cup (60ml) mirin
2 tablespoons honey
1 tablespoon wasabi paste
1 teaspoon sesame oil
300g (9½ ounces) piece sashimi tuna
2 tablespoons (46g) drained pink pickled ginger, sliced thinly

1 Combine sauce, mirin, honey, wasabi and oil in medium bowl;
reserve ½ cup of marinade in small jug. Add tuna to medium bowl;
turn tuna to coat in marinade. Cover; refrigerate 3 hours or overnight.
2 Drain tuna; discard marinade. Cook tuna in heated oiled medium
frying pan until browned both sides and cooked as you like (do not
overcook as tuna has a tendency to dry out). Cut tuna into 24 cubes.
3 Place chinese spoons on serving platter. Place one piece of tuna
in each spoon; top with 1 teaspoon of the reserved marinade and a
little ginger.

prep + cook time 45 minutes (+ refrigeration) **makes** 24
nutritional count per spoon 0.9g total fat (0.3g saturated fat);
138kJ (33 cal); 2.2g carbohydrate; 3.6g protein; 0.1g fibre
tip Chinese spoons are available from Asian food stores.

Duck and green onion gyozas (pot stickers)

1kg (2 pounds) chinese barbecued duck
4 green onions (scallions), sliced thinly
2 tablespoons sake
1 tablespoon japanese soy sauce
2cm (¾-inch) piece fresh ginger (10g), grated
1 fresh long red chilli, chopped finely
30 gyoza wrappers
2 tablespoons vegetable oil
sake dipping sauce
¼ cup (60ml) sake
2 tablespoons japanese soy sauce
1 tablespoon lime juice
1 teaspoon caster (superfine) sugar

1 Discard skin and bones from duck; chop meat finely. Combine duck meat, onion, sake, sauce, ginger and chilli in medium bowl.
2 Place one heaped teaspoon of duck mixture in centre of one wrapper; wet edge around one half of wrapper. Pleat to seal. Repeat with remaining duck mixture and wrappers.
3 Cover base of large frying pan with water; bring to the boil then add gyoza, in batches. Reduce heat; simmer, covered, 3 minutes.
4 Meanwhile, make sake dipping sauce.
5 Heat oil in same cleaned pan; cook gyoza, one side only, uncovered, in batches, until browned and slightly crisp. Drain on absorbent paper. Serve immediately with dipping sauce.
sake dipping sauce Place ingredients in screw-top jar; shake well.

prep + cook time 1 hour 10 minutes **makes** 30
nutritional count per gyoza 3.2g total fat (0.7g saturated fat); 276kJ (66 cal); 3.4g carbohydrate; 5.3g protein; 0.2g fibre

Mini japanese pancakes

4 uncooked large king prawns (shrimp) (280g)
½ cup (75g) plain (all-purpose) flour
½ cup (75g) self-raising flour
tiny pinch bicarbonate of soda (baking soda)
3 eggs
½ cup (125ml) water
2 teaspoons japanese soy sauce
50g (1½ ounces) wombok (napa cabbage), chopped finely
3 green onions (scallions), chopped finely
¼ cup (55g) mayonnaise
1 tablespoon tonkatsu sauce
¼ sheet toasted seaweed (nori), shredded finely

1 Shell and devein prawns; chop finely.
2 Sift flours and soda into medium bowl. Make well in centre; whisk in eggs, water and sauce to make a smooth batter.
3 Stir prawns, wombok and onion into batter.
4 Cook teaspoons of batter, in batches, in large oiled frying pan over medium heat until bubbles appear. Turn pancakes to cook other side. Place on wire rack to cool.
5 Top each pancake with ¼ teaspoon mayonnaise, a drop of tonkatsu and a sprinkling of seaweed. Serve immediately.

prep + cook time 35 minutes **makes** 40
nutritional count per pancake 1g total fat (0.2g saturated fat); 121kJ (29 cal); 3.1g carbohydrate; 1.7g protein; 0.2g fibre
tips Tonkatsu sauce is available ready-made from Asian food stores or you can make your own (see recipe page 291).
Use scissors to finely shred the sheets of seaweed.

Chicken yakitori

500g (1 pound) chicken breast fillets, sliced thinly
½ cup (125ml) mirin
¼ cup (60ml) kecap manis
1 tablespoon japanese soy sauce
1 teaspoon white sesame seeds, toasted
1 green onion (scallion), sliced thinly

1 Thread chicken loosely onto skewers; place, in single layer, in large shallow dish.
2 Combine mirin, kecap manis and sauce in small jug. Pour half the marinade over skewers; reserve remaining marinade. Cover skewers; refrigerate 3 hours or overnight.
3 Simmer reserved marinade in small saucepan over low heat until reduced by half.
4 Meanwhile, cook drained skewers on heated oiled grill plate (or grill or grill pan) until cooked through.
5 Serve skewers drizzled with hot marinade; sprinkle with seeds and onion.

prep + cook time 30 minutes (+ refrigeration) **makes** 24
nutritional count per skewer 0.6g total fat (0.1g saturated fat); 121kJ (29 cal); 0.3g carbohydrate; 4.9g protein; 0g fibre
tip You need 24 bamboo skewers for this recipe. Soak them in cold water for an hour before use to prevent them splintering or scorching during cooking.

Mini crumbed chicken bites

4 chicken breast fillets (800g)
⅔ cup (100g) plain (all-purpose) flour
3 cups (150g) japanese breadcrumbs
3 eggs
vegetable oil, for deep-frying
tonkatsu dipping sauce
⅓ cup (80ml) tonkatsu sauce
1 tablespoon japanese soy sauce
1 tablespoon mirin

1 Place chicken breasts between sheets of plastic wrap. Using meat mallet, pound chicken until 1cm (½-inch) thick. Cut chicken into 3cm (1¼-inch) squares.
2 Place flour and breadcrumbs in separate large, shallow bowls. Beat eggs lightly in another large shallow bowl. Coat chicken in flour; shake away excess. Dip chicken in egg, then in breadcrumbs.
3 Make tonkatsu dipping sauce.
4 Heat oil in large, deep saucepan; deep-fry chicken, in batches, until golden and cooked through; drain on absorbent paper.
5 Serve chicken immediately with dipping sauce.
tonkatsu dipping sauce Bring ingredients to the boil in small saucepan. Reduce heat; simmer, uncovered, 2 minutes.

prep + cook time 40 minutes **makes** 80
nutritional count per bite 1.8g total fat (0.4g saturated fat); 155kJ (37 cal); 2.2g carbohydrate; 2.9g protein; 0.1g fibre
tips You can crumb chicken up to 24 hours in advance. Place in single layer on tray; cover and refrigerate.
Tonkatsu sauce is available ready-made from Asian food stores or you can make your own (see recipe page 291).

Sashimi

Sashimi is usually eaten at the beginning of a meal, presumably before the tastebuds have been dulled by other flavours.

Outside of Japan, the fish to use for sashimi and sushi should be those that are in season and labelled "sashimi quality", as a guarantee of correct health and handling standards. This fish should have a firm texture, a pleasant sea-smell (but not "fishy"), bright red gills and, ideally, bright, clear eyes, although the eyes of a perfectly fresh fish can turn cloudy due to contact with ice.

Either buy whole fish and fillet it yourself, or select fillets or blocks (of tuna) which can then be sliced for you by the fishmonger, if preferred. Fish slices discolour quickly once cut, so it is preferable to slice it as close to serving time as possible. Incidentally, meat from the same tuna can be three different shades of red or pink, depending on which part of the fish it is from.

If you choose to cut the fish yourself, always use a very sharp knife with a long, flexible, very thin blade. Never "saw" the fish; cut it in a single movement, pulling the knife down and towards your body.

Dipping sauces and garnishes are not purely decorative, but enhance the flavour of fish. Daikon aids digestion and cuts the oiliness of the fish, while pickled ginger cleanses the palate between bites of different fish. It is best to place a tiny amount of wasabi directly on each piece of fish and then dip it into the sauce. Mixing wasabi into the dipping sauce only diminishes both flavours.

Tuna sashimi

200g (6½ ounces) daikon, shredded finely
400g (12½-ounce) piece sashimi tuna
2 teaspoons wasabi paste
2 tablespoons (35g) drained pink pickled ginger
⅓ cup (80ml) japanese soy sauce

1 Place daikon in medium bowl, cover with iced water, stand 15 minutes; drain.
2 Place tuna on chopping board; using very sharp knife, cut 6mm (¼-inch) slices at right angle to the grain of the fish, holding piece of skinned fish with your fingers and slicing with knife almost vertical to the board.
3 Divide tuna and daikon among serving plates; serve with wasabi, ginger and sauce.

prep time 10 minutes (+ standing) **serves** 4
nutritional count per serving 2.2g total fat (0.5g saturated fat); 635kJ (152 cal); 4g carbohydrate; 27.8g protein; 0.9g fibre
tip Use a mandoline (if you have one) to shred the daikon.

Sashimi rolls

200g (6½-ounce) piece sashimi fish
½ lebanese cucumber (65g)
1 green onion (scallion), green part only
¼ medium red capsicum (bell pepper) (50g), sliced thinly
¼ cup (60ml) japanese soy sauce

1 Sharpen knife using a steel; wipe knife. Cut fish into paper-thin slices.
2 Halve cucumber lengthways; discard seeds with teaspoon. Cut cucumber and onion into long, thin strips; trim strips to same size as width of fish slices.
3 Place fish slice on board; place one or two pieces of each vegetable at one end. Roll fish to enclose filling. Repeat with remaining fish and filling. Serve rolls with sauce.

prep time 20 minutes **makes** 18
nutritional count per roll 0.2g total fat (0g saturated fat); 67kJ (16 cal); 0.2g carbohydrate; 3.2g protein; 0.1g fibre
tips We used a combination of red (salmon), oily (tuna) and white (snapper) fish for this recipe, but you could also use trevally or various other types so long as all are labelled sashimi-quality at your fishmonger or market. Ask your fishmonger to slice it thinly for you if you prefer not to do so yourself.
When serving mixed sashimi, it is important that the different types of fish do not touch one another.
A toasted nori sheet or a few garlic chives or blanched spinach leaves, can also be used, trimmed to the same size as each piece of fish.

Sashimi salmon with lemon

360g (11½ ounces) daikon, shredded finely
1 small carrot (70g), shredded finely
2 teaspoons wasabi powder
400g (12½-ounce) piece sashimi salmon
1 tablespoon (18g) drained pink pickled ginger
lemon dipping sauce
½ cup (125ml) rice vinegar
¼ cup (55g) caster (superfine) sugar
1 teaspoon light soy sauce
¼ teaspoon finely grated lemon rind
1 green onion (scallion), green part only, chopped finely

1 Place daikon and carrot in separate bowls, cover with iced water; stand 15 minutes. Drain combined daikon and carrot.
2 To make wasabi leaves, add enough water to wasabi to make a soft, spreadable paste; roll level teaspoons into small balls. Flatten; shape with fingers into leaf shape. Lightly mark veins with a small knife or toothpick.
3 Make lemon dipping sauce.
4 Place knife at 45-degree angle to edge of salmon fillet; slice thinly. Cover salmon slices with plastic wrap to prevent drying out. Roll one slice of salmon tightly then wrap three or four salmon slices around upright rolled piece until it resembles a rose. Repeat with remaining salmon to make 12 roses.
5 Divide daikon mixture and salmon roses among serving plates; arrange wasabi leaves around roses. Serve with ginger and lemon dipping sauce.
lemon dipping sauce Stir vinegar, sugar and sauce in small saucepan over heat, without boiling, until sugar dissolves. Remove from heat, add rind; stand 10 minutes. Strain sauce into serving dish; discard rind. Sprinkle sauce with onion.

prep + cook time 25 minutes (+ standing) **serves** 4
nutritional count per serving 13.8g total fat; 1225kJ (293 cal); 17.8g carbohydrate; 23.1g protein; 1.9g fibre

Sashimi tuna and wasabi salad

400g (12½ ounce) piece sashimi tuna
1 medium avocado (250g)
½ cup (150g) japanese mayonnaise
2 teaspoons wasabi paste
½ teaspoon lemon juice
6 green onions (scallions), green part only, sliced thinly
4 iceberg lettuce leaves
1 teaspoon black sesame seeds, toasted
1 tablespoon (25g) drained red pickled ginger

1 Cut tuna and avocado into 1.5cm (¾-inch) cubes. Whisk mayonnaise, wasabi and juice in large bowl until smooth. Add tuna, avocado and all but 2 tablespoons of the onion; toss gently to combine.
2 Divide lettuce leaves among serving bowls; top with tuna mixture. Sprinkle with seeds and remaining onion; serve with ginger.

prep time 15 minutes **serves** 4
nutritional count per serving 36.8g total fat (5.6g saturated fat); 2149kJ (514 cal); 17.4g carbohydrate; 28.2g protein; 1.4g fibre
tip Instead of topping the salad with sesame seeds and green onion, try using finely shredded toasted nori.

Marinated sashimi salmon

500g (1-pound) piece sashimi salmon
2cm (¾-inch) piece fresh ginger (20g), grated
1 clove garlic, crushed
1 teaspoon light brown sugar
2 tablespoons japanese soy sauce
½ cup (125ml) sake
4 green onions (scallions), green part only, chopped finely
2 teaspoons white sesame seeds, toasted

1 Slice salmon into 1cm (½-inch) strips.
2 Combine ginger, garlic, sugar, sauce, sake and half of the onion
in medium bowl; stir until sugar dissolves. Add salmon; stir to coat.
Cover: refrigerate 30 minutes.
3 Mound undrained salmon among serving dishes; sprinkle with seeds
and remaining onion.

prep time 20 minutes (+ refrigeration) **serves** 4
nutritional count per serving 17.7g total fat (0.1g saturated fat);
1258kJ (301 cal); 1.4g carbohydrate; 28.9g protein; 0.3g fibre

Tuna sashimi salad with miso dressing

350g (11-ounce) piece sashimi tuna
2 tablespoons sushi vinegar (see recipe page 98)
4 green onions (scallions), green part only, chopped finely
miso dressing
2 tablespoons white miso
1 tablespoon mirin
1 tablespoon sake
1 tablespoon sugar
2 tablespoons rice vinegar
1 teaspoon japanese soy sauce
¼ teaspoon japanese mustard

1 Cut tuna into 2cm (¾-inch) cubes or slice thinly. Place tuna in medium bowl with vinegar; stand 15 minutes.
2 Meanwhile, make miso dressing.
3 Drain tuna; discard marinade. Pat tuna dry with absorbent paper. Place tuna in medium bowl with chilled dressing; toss gently to coat.
4 Divide tuna mixture among serving bowls; sprinkle with onion. Serve with wasabi or japanese mustard, if you like.
miso dressing Stir miso, mirin, sake and sugar in small saucepan over heat, without boiling, until sugar dissolves. Remove from heat; stand 10 minutes. Stir in vinegar, sauce and mustard. Cover; refrigerate until required.

prep + cook time 25 minutes (+ standing) **serves** 4
nutritional count per serving 2.3g total fat (0.5g saturated fat); 652kJ (156 cal); 7.2g carbohydrate; 24.6g protein; 0.7g fibre
tip Sashimi salmon may be used instead of tuna.

Sashimi stacks

½ sheet toasted seaweed (yaki-nori)
½ lebanese cucumber (65g)
½ medium avocado (125g)
400g (12½-ounce) piece sashimi salmon
1 teaspoon wasabi paste
4 green onions (scallions), quartered lengthways
2 teaspoons white sesame seeds, toasted
2 tablespoons japanese soy sauce

1 Cut seaweed into 16 strips.
2 Halve cucumber lengthways; discard seeds with teaspoon.
Cut cucumber and avocado into long, thin strips.
3 Cut salmon into 32 thin slices. Place 16 slices of the salmon
in single layer on serving platter; spread each with a little wasabi.
Top with cucumber, avocado and onion; finish with remaining
salmon slices.
4 Wrap seaweed strip around each stack; sprinkle with seeds.
Serve stacks with sauce.

prep time 30 minutes **makes** 16
nutritional count per stack 4.8g total fat (0.3g saturated fat);
284kJ (68 cal); 0.2g carbohydrate; 5.9g protein; 0.2g fibre

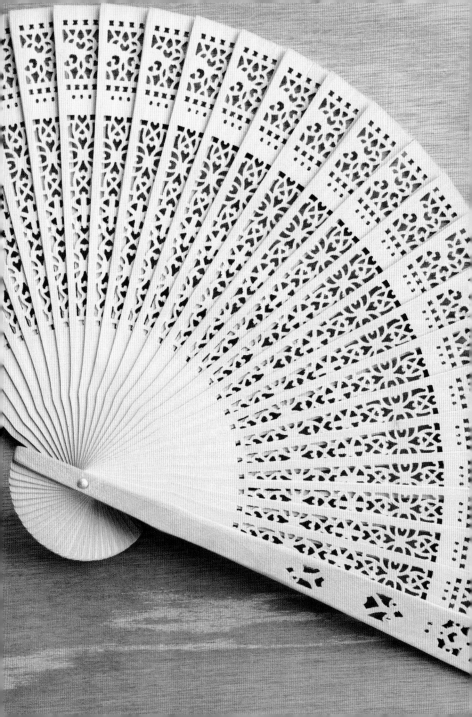

Sushi

Sushi rice

3 cups (600g) japanese rice (koshihikari)
3 cups (750ml) water
sushi vinegar
½ cup (125ml) rice vinegar
¼ cup (55g) sugar
½ teaspoon salt

1 Place rice in large bowl, cover with cold water, stir with hand. Drain; repeat process two or three times until water is almost clear. Drain rice in strainer at least 30 minutes.
2 Meanwhile, make sushi vinegar.
3 Place rice and the water in medium saucepan, cover tightly; bring to the boil. Reduce heat; simmer, covered tightly, on low heat about 12 minutes or until water is absorbed. Remove from heat; allow rice to stand, covered, 10 minutes.
4 Spread rice in large, non-metallic flat-based bowl or tub (preferably wood). Using large flat wooden spoon or plastic spatula, repeatedly slice through rice at sharp angle to break up lumps and separate grains, gradually pouring in sushi vinegar. Not all of the vinegar may be required; rice shouldn't become too wet or mushy. Continue to slice through the rice (don't stir because it crushes the rice grains) with one hand, lifting and turning rice from outside into centre.
5 Meanwhile, using other hand, fan rice until it is almost cool; this will take about 5 minutes (an electric fan, on the low setting, can be used instead of a hand-held fan if you prefer). Do not over-cool rice or it will harden. Performing these two actions together will give you glossy, slightly sticky but still separate sushi rice. Keep rice covered with damp cloth to stop it drying out while making sushi.
sushi vinegar Stir ingredients in small bowl until sugar dissolves. (For a slightly less stringent mixture, heat it gently just before using.)

prep + cook time 25 minutes (+ standing) **makes** 9 cups
nutritional count per 1 cup 0.3g total fat (0.1g saturated fat); 1091kJ (261 cal); 58.8g carbohydrate; 4.4g protein; 0.5g fibre
tips Sushi vinegar can be made ahead; refrigerate in an airtight container. You could also use ½ cup (125ml) ready-made bottled sushi vinegar.

Tuna rolls

3 sheets toasted seaweed (yaki-nori)
3 cups prepared sushi rice (see recipe page 98)
1 tablespoon wasabi paste
200g (6½-ounce) piece sashimi tuna, cut into thick strips
2 tablespoons (46g) drained pink pickled ginger
¼ cup (60ml) japanese soy sauce

1 Fold one sheet of seaweed in half lengthways, parallel with lines on rough side; cut along fold. Place a half sheet, shiny-side down, lengthways across bamboo mat about 2cm (¾-inch) from side closest to you.
2 Dip fingers in bowl of rice vinegared water (see tip), shake off excess; pick up about ½ cup of the rice, squeeze into oblong shape, place across centre of seaweed. Wet fingers again, then gently "rake" rice evenly from left to right, leaving 2cm (¾-inch) border on far end of seaweed. Build up rice in front of border to form a mound to keep filling in place.
3 Swipe a dab of wasabi across centre of rice, flattening it out evenly. Place tuna strips, end to end, in a row over wasabi across centre of rice.
4 Starting with side closest to you, pick up mat using thumb and index fingers of both hands; use remaining fingers to hold filling in place as you begin to roll mat away from you. Roll forward, pressing gently but tightly, wrapping seaweed around rice and filling. With roll seam-side down, gentle press it slightly into a square shape
5 Unroll mat; place sushi roll, seam-side down, on board. Wipe very sharp knife with damp cloth then cut roll in half. Turn one piece around so that the two cut ends of each half are aligned. Cut rolls together into third, wiping knife between each cut, to give a total of six pieces.
6 Working quickly, repeat process with remaining seaweed halves, rice and tuna, using a dab of wasabi with each.
7 Serve tuna rolls with remaining wasabi, pickled ginger and sauce.

prep time 20 minutes **makes** 36
nutritional count per roll 0.2g total fat (0.1g saturated fat); 130kJ (31 cal); 5.2g carbohydrate; 1.9g protein; 0.1g fibre
tip For rice vinegared water, add 1 tablespoon rice vinegar to medium bowl of water.

Large spiral rolls

1 lebanese cucumber (130g)
4 sheets toasted seaweed
(yaki-nori)
4 cups prepared sushi rice
(see recipe page 98)
2 tablespoons wasabi paste
4 long, thin strips pickled daikon
200g (6½-ounce) piece sashimi
tuna, cut into 1cm (½-inch) strips

½ quantity thick omelette
(see recipe page 61),
cut into wide strips
4 strips seasoned gourd (kampyo)
¼ cup (20g) dried flaked cod
2 tablespoons (46g) drained
pink pickled ginger
¼ cup (60ml) japanese soy sauce

1 Halve cucumber lengthways; discard seeds with teaspoon. Cut into strips. Place one sheet of seaweed, shiny-side down, lengthways across bamboo mat about 2cm (¾-inch) from side closest to you.
2 Dip fingers in bowl of rice vinegared water (see tip), shake off excess; place about a quarter of the rice across centre of seaweed. Wet fingers again, then gently "rake" rice evenly from left to right leaving 2cm (¾-inch) border on far side of seaweed. Build up rice in front of border to form a mound to keep filling in place.
3 Swipe a dab of wasabi across centre of rice, flattening it out evenly. Place about a quarter of the pickled daikon, tuna, cucumber, omelette, gourd and dried cod in a row over wasabi; ensure fillings extend to both ends of rice.
4 Starting with side closest to you, pick up mat using thumb and index fingers of both hands; use remaining fingers to hold filling in place as you begin to roll mat away from you. Roll forward, pressing gently but tightly, wrapping seaweed around rice and fillings. With roll seam-side down, gentle press it slightly into a square shape.
5 Unroll mat; place sushi roll, seam-side down, on board. Wipe very sharp knife with damp cloth then cut roll in half. Turn one piece around so that the two cut ends of each half are aligned. Slice rolls together in half then in half again, wiping knife between each cut, for a total of eight pieces.
6 Working quickly, repeat process with remaining seaweed, rice and filling ingredients, using a dab of wasabi with each.
7 Serve rolls with remaining wasabi, pickled ginger and sauce.

prep time 20 minutes **makes** 32
nutritional count per roll 0.7g total fat (0.2g saturated fat); 209kJ (50 cal); 7.8g carbohydrate; 2.8g protein; 0.2g fibre
tip For rice vinegared water, add 1 tablespoon rice vinegar to bowl of water.

Inside-out rolls

4 cooked medium king prawns (shrimp) (180g)
½ lebanese cucumber (65g)
2 sheets toasted seaweed (yaki-nori)
4 cups prepared sushi rice (see recipe page 98)
2 tablespoons flying fish roe
1 teaspoon black sesame seeds, toasted
1½ tablespoons wasabi paste
4 long, thin strips pickled daikon
1½ tablespoons (35g) drained red pickled ginger
2 tablespoons (46g) drained pink pickled ginger
¼ cup (60ml) japanese soy sauce

1 Shell and devein prawns; halve lengthways. Halve cucumber lengthways; discard seeds with teaspoon. Cut cucumber into thin strips.
2 Fold one sheet of seaweed in half lengthways, parallel with lines on rough side; cut along fold. Place a half sheet lengthways across bamboo mat about 2cm (¾-inch) from side of mat closest to you.
3 Dip fingers in bowl of rice vinegared water (see tip), shake off excess; pick up a quarter of the rice, press onto seaweed then gently "rake" rice evenly from left to right to cover seaweed completely. Sprinkle a quarter of the roe and seeds over rice then cover with plastic wrap. Carefully lift mat; turn over so nori faces up; place back on bamboo mat about 2cm (¾-inch) from the edge. Swipe a dab of wasabi across centre of nori, then top with about a quarter of the cucumber, prawn, daikon and red ginger, extending filling to both ends of nori.
4 Pick up the edge of the bamboo mat and plastic wrap with index finger and thumb; place remaining fingers on filling to hold in place as you roll mat tightly away from you, wrapping rice around filling. Press roll gently and continue rolling to complete roll. Unroll mat; keep roll in plastic wrap.
5 Wipe sharp knife with damp cloth; cut roll, still in plastic wrap, in half, then each half into quarters, to make eight pieces, wiping knife between each cut. Remove plastic wrap and serve rolls with remaining wasabi, pink ginger and sauce.

prep time 20 minutes **makes** 32
nutritional count per roll 0.3g total fat (0.1g saturated fat); 176kJ (42 cal); 8g carbohydrate; 1.6g protein; 0.2g fibre
tips Make two small cuts in the underside of the prawns so they lie flat. For rice vinegared water, add 1 tablespoon rice vinegar to bowl of water.

Sushi hand rolls

1 lebanese cucumber (130g)
3 cups prepared sushi rice (see recipe page 98)
4 sheets toasted seaweed (yaki-nori)
1 large avocado (320g)
1 tablespoon lemon juice
2 tablespoons mayonnaise
1 teaspoon wasabi paste
4 japanese seafood sticks, quartered lengthways
1 teaspoon black sesame seeds, toasted
½ cup (125ml) japanese soy sauce
2 tablespoons (46g) drained pink pickled ginger

1 Halve cucumber lengthways; discard seeds with teaspoon.
Cut into 16 strips.
2 Place rice in non-metallic bowl; cover with damp cloth. Cut each sheet
of seaweed into quarters; cover with plastic wrap until ready to serve.
Slice avocado thinly, brush with lemon juice to stop it discolouring; cover.
Combine mayonnaise and wasabi in small bowl; cover.
3 Place a piece of seaweed, shiny-side down, diagonally across palm of
one hand. Dip fingers of other hand in bowl of vinegared water (see tip),
shake off excess water; pick up about 2 tablespoons of the rice, place
in centre of seaweed, then "rake" rice towards top corner of seaweed,
making a slight groove down the middle of the rice for the filling.
4 Using finger, swipe a dab of wasabi mayonnaise along the groove,
topping it with a slice each of avocado, seafood stick and cucumber,
then a small sprinkle of seeds. Fold one side of seaweed over to
stick to rice; fold other side of seaweed over the first to form a cone.
(Tip of cone can be folded back to hold cone shape securely.)
5 Repeat process with remaining seaweed pieces, rice, mayonnaise,
avocado, seafood stick, cucumber and seeds to make 16 rolls in total.
6 Dip rolls in sauce; top with a slice of pickled ginger and eat immediately.

prep time 30 minutes **makes** 16
nutritional count per roll 4.3g total fat (0.8g saturated fat);
443kJ (106 cal); 13.6g carbohydrate; 2.8g protein; 0.6g fibre
tip For rice vinegared water, add 1 tablespoon rice vinegar to medium
bowl of cold water.

Hand-moulded sushi

3 cups prepared sushi rice (see recipe page 98)
350g (11-ounce) piece sashimi tuna, sliced thinly
2 teaspoons wasabi paste
¼ cup (60ml) japanese soy sauce

1 Dip fingers in bowl of vinegared water (see tip), shake off excess; pick up about 1 tablespoon of rice with one hand, gently squeezing and shaping it into a rectangle shape with rounded edges.
2 Pick up one slice of fish with index finger and thumb of left hand. Using tip of right-hand index finger, scoop up a dab of wasabi; spread wasabi along centre of fish.
3 Bend fingers of left hand to form cup to hold fish; place rice shape on fish. Move left thumb to top end of rice shape to stop rice being pushed off fish; use right-hand index and middle fingers to gently push rice shape and fish together.
4 Turn sushi piece over in left hand so fish is on top, gently push fish against rice with right-hand index and middle fingers; left thumb should remain at top end of rice to stop it being pushed out.
5 With thumb on one side of rice and index finger on the other, gently squeeze rice to straighten the sides.
6 Using right-hand index finger and thumb, turn sushi 180 degrees and push fish against rice again with right-hand index and middle fingers.
7 Serve sushi with sauce.

prep time 20 minutes **makes** 30
nutritional count per piece 0.3g total fat (0.1g saturated fat); 171kJ (41 cal); 5.9g carbohydrate; 3.6g protein; 0.1g fibre
tips For rice vinegared water, add 1 tablespoon rice vinegar to medium bowl of cold water.
To keep fish on rice, place a 1cm (½-inch) wide strip of toasted seaweed (yaki-nori) around centre of sushi piece with ends tucked underneath; moisture from the rice will hold seaweed in place.
Don't make the pieces too big; each should only make a single mouthful. It correctly formed, hand-moulded sushi should be able to be eaten upside down using fingers, or on its side if eaten with chopsticks; it's the fish and not the rice which is to be dipped in soy sauce.

Seasoned tofu pouches

1 lebanese cucumber (130g)
8 seasoned fried bean curd pouches
1 teaspoon black sesame seeds, toasted
1½ cups prepared sushi rice (see recipe page 98)
8 strips seasoned gourd (seasoned kampyo)
1 teaspoon (5g) drained red pickled ginger

1 Halve cucumber lengthways; discard seeds with teaspoon. Dice.
2 Carefully cut open pouches on one side, gently pushing fingers into each corner to form pouch.
3 Reserve a few of the seeds for garnish; fold remaining seeds and cucumber through rice.
4 Dip fingers of right hand in bowl of vinegared water, shake off excess; pick up about an eighth of the rice with right hand, gently and loosely fill one pouch, being careful not to overfill or tear pouch and to push rice into corners.
5 Fold one side of pouch down over rice; fold other side over to enclose filling. Turn pouch over so join is underneath.
6 Tie a strip of gourd around pouch with a loose knot on top; repeat with remaining ingredients. Garnish with a little red pickled ginger and reserved sesame seeds.

prep + cook time 30 minutes **makes** 8
nutritional count per pouch 7.4g total fat (1.3g saturated fat); 677kJ (162 cal); 12g carbohydrate; 11.3g protein; 0.7g fibre
tips Ready-made seasoned bean-curd skins and seasoned gourd (kampyo) strips are available from Asian specialist grocery stores.
For rice vinegared water, add 1 tablespoon rice vinegar to medium bowl of cold water.

California rolls

1 egg
1 teaspoon sake
1 teaspoon oil
2 sheets toasted seaweed (yaki-nori)
3 cups prepared sushi rice (see recipe page 98)
2 crab sticks (40g), cut into strips
25g (¾ ounce) pickled daikon, cut into strips
4cm piece carrot (25g), cut into strips
4cm piece cucumber (25g), cut into strips
¼ cup (60ml) japanese soy sauce
2 tablespoons (46g) drained pink pickled ginger
2 teaspoons wasabi paste

1 Lightly beat egg and sake in small bowl until combined. Heat oil in wok. Pour egg mixture into wok; cook, tilting wok, until egg is almost set. Remove omelette from wok; roll tightly, slice thinly. Cool to room temperature.
2 Place one sheet of seaweed, shiny-side down, on sushi mat. Using damp fingers, spread half the rice over seaweed, leaving 4cm (1¾-inch) border at one end.
3 Layer omelette, crab, daikon, carrot and cucumber over centre of rice.
4 Using mat, roll firmly to form sushi roll. Place roll, seam-side down, on board; using sharp knife, cut roll into six mini-maki pieces.
5 Repeat with remaining seaweed, rice, omelette, crab, daikon, carrot and cucumber. Serve with sauce, ginger and wasabi.

prep + cook time 30 minutes (+ standing) **makes** 12
nutritional count per roll 1.1g total fat (0.3g saturated fat); 364kJ (87 cal); 16.1g carbohydrate; 2.5g protein; 0.4g fibre

Soups

Primary dashi

10cm (4-inch) piece kelp (konbu)
1 litre (4 cups) water
15g (½ ounce) large smoked dried bonito flakes

1 Wipe kelp with damp cloth; cut into three or four large pieces.
Place kelp pieces in large saucepan with the water; cook, uncovered,
10 minutes or until just about to come to the boil. Remove kelp before
mixture comes to the boil.
2 Bring water to the boil; add an extra ¼ cup (60ml) water and bonito
flakes. Bring to the boil; remove from heat immediately.
3 Allow bonito flakes to settle on base of saucepan; strain through
muslin-lined sieve into large bowl. Reserve kelp and bonito flakes for
making secondary dashi.

prep + cook time 15 minutes **makes** 1 litre (4 cups)
nutritional count per 1 cup 0.5g total fat (0.3g saturated fat);
96kJ (23 cal); 1.5g carbohydrate; 2.8g protein; 0g fibre
tips This light stock is used for clear soups and some dipping sauces.
Do not discard kelp or bonito flakes if intending to make secondary dashi
(see recipe page 117).
Refrigerate leftover primary dashi for up to three days or freeze for up
to one month (but some of its delicate flavour and aroma will be lost).
Freeze in measured amounts, such as 1 cup, or in ice-cube trays.
To make instant primary dashi, stir 1½ teaspoons dashi granules through
1 litre (4 cups) warm water until dissolved.

Secondary dashi

reserved kelp (konbu) and smoked dried bonito flakes
    from primary dashi (see recipe page 116)
1.5 litres (6 cups) water
10g (½ ounce) large smoked dried bonito flakes, extra

1 Place reserved kelp and bonito flakes in large saucepan with the
water; cook, uncovered, 10 minutes or until just about to come to
the boil. Reduce heat; simmer, uncovered, about 15 minutes or until
reduced by half.
2 Add extra bonito flakes; remove from heat. Allow bonito flakes
to settle on base of saucepan; strain through muslin-lined sieve into
large bowl.

prep + cook time 25 minutes **makes** 3 cups
nutritional count per 1 cup 1g total fat (0.5g saturated fat);
188kJ (45 cal); 3.1g carbohydrate; 5.6g protein; 0g fibre
tips This is a heavier stock than the primary dashi. It is used in thick and
miso soups, seasoned stocks and simmered dishes, where a stronger
flavour is required.
Refrigerate leftover secondary dashi for up to three days or freeze for
up to one month (but some of its delicate flavour and aroma will be lost).
Freeze in measured amounts, such as 1 cup, or in ice-cube trays.
To make instant secondary dashi, stir 2 teaspoons dashi granules through
1 litre (4 cups) warm water until dissolved.

Pork and green bean miso soup

1 litre (4 cups) secondary dashi (see recipe page 117)
100g (3 ounces) pork fillet, sliced thinly
8 green beans, cut into small chunks
¼ cup (75g) red miso
2 teaspoons fresh ginger juice
2 green onions (scallions), chopped finely

1 Bring dashi to the boil in medium saucepan. Add pork and beans;
return to the boil. Reduce heat; simmer, uncovered, 2 minutes.
2 Place miso in small bowl; gradually add 1 cup of the hot dashi, stirring,
until miso dissolves. Add to saucepan; stir to combine. Bring to the boil;
remove immediately from heat. Stir in juice.
3 Serve soup sprinkled with onion.

prep + cook time 25 minutes **serves** 4
nutritional count per serving 2.3g total fat (0.6g saturated fat);
368kJ (88 cal); 6.2g carbohydrate; 10.8g protein; 1.4g fibre
tips Don't overcook the soup after the miso is added or some of the
delicate flavour will be lost.
To obtain ginger juice, squeeze grated fresh ginger into a sieve set over
a bowl. A piece of ginger measuring about 10cm (4 inches) in length will
yield 2 tablespoons of grated ginger; this amount of grated ginger should
in turn yield the 2 teaspoons of juice used in this recipe.

Vegetable soup

60g (2 ounces) daikon
1 small potato (120g)
1 small carrot (70g)
2 teaspoons vegetable oil
1 litre (4 cups) secondary dashi (see recipe page 117)
1½ tablespoons japanese soy sauce
2 green onions (scallions), cut into chunks
60g (2 ounces) green beans, cut into chunks
2 fresh shiitake mushrooms, quartered
½ x 227g (7 ounces) can sliced bamboo shoots, rinsed, drained
1 teaspoon seven-spice mix

1 Quarter daikon and potato; slice thinly. Halve carrot lengthways; slice thinly.
2 Heat oil in large saucepan; cook daikon, potato and carrot, stirring, until browned lightly.
3 Add dashi and sauce; bring to the boil. Reduce heat; simmer, uncovered, about 5 minutes or until carrot is tender. Add onion, beans, mushrooms and shoots; simmer, uncovered until vegetables are tender.
4 Serve soup sprinkled with seven-spice mix.

prep + cook time 25 minutes **serves** 4
nutritional count per serving 2.9g total fat (0.5g saturated fat);
330kJ (79 cal); 7g carbohydrate; 4.8g protein; 2g fibre
tips You can substitute chicken stock for dashi.
You can add 100g (3 ounces) tofu or 150g (5 ounces) minced pork or chicken if you want to make this soup more substantial.

Poached chicken in citrus wakame broth

5g (½ ounce) dried seaweed (wakame)
1 litre (4 cups) chicken stock
2 cups (500ml) water
2 chicken breast fillets (400g)
2.5cm (1-inch) piece fresh ginger (15g), sliced thinly
1 fresh small red thai chilli (serrano chili), sliced thinly
2 cloves garlic, sliced thinly
2 kaffir lime leaves, torn
100g (3 ounces) dried soba noodles
½ cup (40g) bean sprouts, trimmed
2 tablespoons fish sauce
⅓ cup (80ml) lime juice
2 baby buk choy (300g), leaves separated

1 Place seaweed in small bowl, cover with cold water; stand 10 minutes; drain. Chop coarsely, removing any hard ribs or stems.
2 Bring stock, the water, chicken, ginger, chilli, garlic and lime leaves to the boil in large saucepan. Reduce heat; simmer, uncovered, about 10 minutes or until cooked through. Cool chicken in broth 10 minutes; remove from pan. Strain broth through muslin-lined sieve over large bowl; discard solids, return broth to pan. Slice chicken thinly.
3 Meanwhile, cook noodles in large saucepan of boiling water until tender; drain. Divide noodles, seaweed and sprouts among bowls.
4 Bring broth to the boil; reduce heat and stir in sauce, juice and buk choy. Ladle broth over noodles; top with chicken and lime wedges, if you like.

prep + cook time 50 minutes **serves** 4
nutritional count per serving 3.9g total fat (1.2g saturated fat); 1053kJ (252 cal); 20.9g carbohydrate; 30.7g protein; 3.3g fibre

Udon noodle soup

1.5 litres (6 cups) water
3 teaspoons dashi granules
2 small leeks (400g), sliced thinly
3 spring onions
200g (6½ ounces) pork loin, sliced thinly
⅓ cup (80ml) japanese soy sauce
2 tablespoons mirin
400g (12½ ounces) dried udon noodles

1 Bring the water and dashi granules to the boil in large saucepan; add leek, return to the boil. Reduce heat; simmer, uncovered, about 5 minutes or until tender.
2 Meanwhile, cut 2 spring onions into chunks; thinly slice remaining onion. Add onion chunks, pork, sauce and mirin to pan; simmer until pork is cooked through.
3 Cook noodles in large saucepan of boiling water until tender; drain.
4 Divide noodles and soup among bowls; sprinkle with sliced onion. Serve sprinkled with a little seven-spice mix, if you like.

prep + cook time 15 minutes **serves** 4
nutritional count per serving 3.3g total fat (0.9g saturated fat); 1822kJ (436 cal); 71.9g carbohydrate; 24.4g protein; 5.3g fibre
tip Be careful to not overcook the pork. It will cook very quickly if sliced thinly.

Clear soup with prawns and spinach

4 uncooked medium king prawns (shrimp) (180g)
50g (1½ ounces) baby spinach leaves
4 large strips lemon rind
1 litre (4 cups) primary dashi (see recipe page 116)
2 teaspoons light soy sauce

1 Shell and devein prawns, leaving tails intact. Slit underside of prawns; press flat. Cut small slit in centre of each prawn; push tail through slit.
2 Cook prawns in small saucepan of boiling water, uncovered, 1 minute or until just changed in colour; drain on absorbent paper.
3 Boil, steam or microwave spinach until wilted; rinse under cold water, drain. Squeeze out excess moisture.
4 Starting at opposite ends of a rectangular strip of rind, cut slits along both long sides, not quite through to the other end; twist to form an open triangle. Repeat with remaining strips of rind.
5 Bring dashi to the boil in medium saucepan; stir in sauce.
6 Divide spinach and prawns, tails facing up, among serving bowls; ladle over soup. Top with rind triangles.

prep + cook time 35 minutes **serves** 4
nutritional count per serving 0.7g total fat (0.3g saturated fat); 196kJ (47 cal); 1.8g carbohydrate; 7.9g protein; 0.4g fibre
tips The method used to create the lemon-rind triangles can also be used successfully with limes, oranges, cucumber and carrot.
An easy way to handle hot wilted spinach without burning yourself is to lay it across a bamboo sushi mat, roll firmly and squeeze to remove excess moisture.

Clear soup with tofu and wakame

5g (¼ ounce) dried seaweed (wakame)
200g (6½ ounces) firm tofu, cut into 8 slices
1 litre (4 cups) primary dashi (see recipe page 116)
1 tablespoon sake
2 teaspoons light soy sauce
1 teaspoon finely shredded lemon rind

1 Place seaweed in small bowl, cover with cold water, stand 5 minutes; drain, squeezing out any excess moisture. Coarsely chop seaweed, removing any hard ribs.
2 Meanwhile, cut eight 3.5cm (1½-inch) flower shapes from tofu slices.
3 Divide seaweed and tofu among bowls.
4 Bring dashi to the boil in medium saucepan; stir in sake and sauce. Ladle over tofu; sprinkle with rind.

prep + cook time 25 minutes **serves** 4
nutritional count per serving 4.2g total fat (0.8g saturated fat); 389kJ (93 cal); 1.6g carbohydrate; 9.2g protein; 4.2g fibre
tips If you don't own a flower cutter, cut tofu into 1.5cm (¾-inch) cubes. Use a citrus zester to make long, very fine shreds of lemon rind.

Ramen noodles with soy broth

8 dried shiitake mushrooms
500g (1 pound) fresh ramen
noodles
⅓ cup (80ml) japanese soy sauce
⅓ cup (80ml) sake
100g (3 ounces) bamboo shoots,
sliced thinly
125g (4 ounces) chinese
barbecued pork, sliced thinly
500g (1 pound) baby buk choy,
leaves separated, blanched
1 cup (80g) bean sprouts, trimmed
4 green onions (scallions),
cut into chunks

soy broth
1kg (2 pounds) pork bones
1kg (2 pounds) chicken bones
10 spring onion bulbs, bruised
100g (3 ounces) fresh ginger,
sliced
1 head garlic, halved widthways
2 medium carrots (240g),
cut into chunks
10cm (4-inch) piece kelp (konbu)

1 Make soy broth.
2 Place mushrooms in small heatproof bowl, cover with boiling water, stand 20 minutes; drain. Discard stems.
3 Cook noodles in large saucepan of boiling water, until tender; drain. Rinse under cold water; drain.
4 Bring broth, sauce and sake to the boil in large saucepan.
5 Divide noodles and broth among bowls; top with mushrooms and remaining ingredients. Serve with seven-spice mix and chilli sesame oil, if you like.
soy broth Place bones in large saucepan; cover with water. Bring to the boil; drain. Rinse bones; return to saucepan. Add remaining ingredients; cover with water by 5cm (2 inches). Bring to the boil; remove and discard seaweed. Simmer about 5 hours or until liquid has reduced to 1.5 litres (6 cups); strain into large bowl. Refrigerate broth until cold; discard fat from surface.

prep + cook time 6 hours (+ standing & refrigeration) **serves** 4
nutritional count per serving 6.5g total fat (2.5g saturated fat); 1317kJ (315 cal); 38.4g carbohydrate; 19.1g protein; 6.1g fibre
tips To help the kelp release its flavour, make a few cuts along the edge with a pair of scissors.
It's best to make the broth the day before. The broth needs to chill long enough for the fat to solidify on top; discard the fat.

Salmon and shiitake soup

1kg (2 pounds) salmon bones and heads
1 small brown onion (80g), quartered
1.25 litres (5 cups) water
¼ cup (60g) white miso
4 fresh shiitake mushrooms, sliced thinly
2 teaspoons fresh ginger juice
16 snow pea sprouts, trimmed
80g (2½ ounces) daikon, shredded finely

1 Place salmon bones and heads in large saucepan with onion and the water. Bring to the boil. Reduce heat; simmer, uncovered, 20 minutes. Remove any scum from surface of stock. Strain stock mixture through muslin-lined strainer into large bowl. Return stock to same cleaned pan.
2 Place miso in small bowl, gradually add 1 cup (250ml) of the hot stock, stirring, until miso dissolves. Add to saucepan, stir to combine.
3 Add mushrooms, return to a simmer. Remove from heat; stir in juice. Serve soup topped with sprouts and daikon.

prep + cook time 40 minutes **serves** 4
nutritional count per serving 1.7g total fat (0.5g saturated fat); 288kJ (69 cal); 6.4g carbohydrate; 6.1g protein; 1.6g fibre
tips For a stronger flavour, simmer the stock after straining to intensify its flavour.
You can use red miso instead of white. Red miso is stronger and saltier, so only use about 2 tablespoons in this recipe.
To obtain ginger juice, squeeze grated fresh ginger into a sieve set over a bowl. A piece of ginger measuring about 10cm (4 inches) in length will yield 2 tablespoons of grated ginger; this amount of grated ginger should in turn yield the 2 teaspoons of juice used in this recipe.

Egg drop soup

1 litre (4 cups) primary dashi (see recipe page 116)
1 tablespoon mirin
1 tablespoon light soy sauce
2 teaspoons japanese soy sauce
2 eggs, beaten lightly
2 green onions (scallions), sliced thinly

1 Bring dashi to the boil in large saucepan. Stir in mirin and sauces; gradually stir in egg.
2 Serve soup sprinkled with onion.

prep + cook time 10 minutes **serves** 4
nutritional count per serving 3.5g total fat (1.2g saturated fat); 297kJ (71 cal); 2g carbohydrate; 7g protein; 0g fibre
tip You can add 100g (3 ounces) cooked green beans for a more substantial soup, if you like.

Ramen, pork and spinach soup

1kg (2 pounds) chicken necks
3 litres (12 cups) water
1 large leek (500g), chopped coarsely
5cm (2-inch) piece fresh ginger (25g), sliced thinly
10 black peppercorns
250g (8 ounces) fresh ramen noodles
¼ cup (60ml) japanese soy sauce
¼ cup (60ml) sake
1 teaspoon sesame oil
300g (9½ ounces) spinach, trimmed, chopped coarsely
200g (6½ ounces) chinese barbecued pork, sliced thinly
1 fresh long red chilli, sliced thinly
½ sheet toasted seaweed (yaki-nori), cut into small pieces

1 Bring chicken, the water, leek, ginger and peppercorns to the boil in large saucepan. Reduce heat; simmer, uncovered, 1 hour. Strain broth through muslin-lined sieve into large heatproof bowl; discard solids. Allow broth to cool; cover. Refrigerate until cold.
2 Discard fat from surface of broth; return broth to same cleaned pan, bring to the boil. Stir in sauce, sake and oil; return to the boil. Remove from heat.
3 Meanwhile, cook noodles in large saucepan of boiling water until tender; drain. Rinse under cold water; drain.
4 Divide noodles, spinach, pork, chilli and seaweed among bowls; ladle over broth.

prep + cook time 1 hour 35 minutes (+ refrigeration) **serves** 4
nutritional count per serving 12.4g total fat (4.8g saturated fat); 1680kJ (402 cal); 40.1g carbohydrate; 26.6g protein; 4.5g fibre
tip It's best to make the broth the day before. The broth needs to chill long enough for the fat to solidify on top; discard the fat.

Somen and dashi broth

3 dried shiitake mushrooms
100g (3 ounces) dried somen noodles
1.5 litres (6 cups) water
2 tablespoons sake
2 tablespoons mirin
2 tablespoons light soy sauce
2 teaspoons dashi granules
2 tablespoons finely shredded lemon rind

1 Place mushrooms in small heatproof bowl, cover with boiling water, stand 20 minutes; drain. Discard stems; slice caps thinly.
2 Meanwhile, cook noodles in medium saucepan of boiling water until tender; drain.
3 Bring the water, sake, mirin, sauce and granules to the boil in large saucepan. Reduce heat; simmer, uncovered, 10 minutes.
4 Divide noodles, mushrooms and rind among bowls; ladle over broth.

prep + cook time 20 minutes **serves** 6
nutritional count per serving 0.2g total fat (0g saturated fat); 297kJ (71 cal); 12.1g carbohydrate; 2.3g protein; 0.7g fibre
tips You can add extra ingredients to this soup: sliced snow peas or green beans, finely grated daikon or kumara, or bean sprouts and tofu. Use a citrus zester to make long, very fine shreds of lemon rind.

Beef and rice soup

1.25 litres (5 cups) primary dashi (see recipe page 116)
3 teaspoons light soy sauce
4 cups hot cooked japanese rice (koshihikari)
150g (5½ ounces) lean beef fillet, cut into paper-thin slices
2 teaspoons white sesame seeds, toasted
2 green onions (scallions), chopped finely
1 tablespoon wasabi paste

1 Bring dashi and sauce to the boil in medium saucepan.
2 Divide hot rice among serving bowls; top with beef, seeds and onion.
Ladle over dashi mixture, taking care not to dislodge the arrangement;
serve with wasabi.

prep + cook time 20 minutes **serves** 4
nutritional count per serving 4.2g total fat (1.5g saturated fat);
1195kJ (286 cal); 45.1g carbohydrate; 15.6g protein; 1g fibre
tips Freeze beef, wrapped in plastic wrap, for about an hour to make it
easier to slice thinly. If sliced thin enough, the beef will cook in the hot
dashi mixture. You can also brown unsliced beef in medium frying pan
to add extra flavour to soup.
You will need to cook 1½ cups (300g) japanese rice to make the amount
required for this recipe.
White fish fillets can be used instead of beef, and seven-spice mix or
chilli can be used instead of the wasabi. In Japan, green tea is sometimes
used for the broth instead of dashi.

Beef with ramen and mushrooms

8 dried shiitake mushrooms
2 tablespoons peanut oil
500g (1 pound) beef strips
4 green onions (scallions), sliced thinly
2 cloves garlic, crushed
2cm (¾-inch) piece fresh ginger (10g), grated
1 litre (4 cups) beef stock
3 cups (750ml) water
1 tablespoon light soy sauce
2 tablespoons rice wine
180g (5½ ounces) fresh ramen noodles

1 Place mushrooms in small heatproof bowl, cover with boiling water; stand 20 minutes, drain. Discard stems; slice caps thinly.
2 Heat half of the oil in large saucepan; cook beef, in batches, until browned all over. Remove from pan.
3 Heat remaining oil in same pan; cook half the onion with garlic and ginger, stirring, until onion softens. Add stock, the water, sauce and wine; bring to the boil.
4 Add mushrooms, beef and noodles; bring to the boil. Reduce heat; simmer, uncovered, about 5 minutes or until noodles are tender.
5 Divide soup among serving bowls; sprinkle with remaining onion.

prep + cook time 30 minutes (+ standing) **serves** 4
nutritional count per serving 21.8g total fat (6.8g saturated fat); 1747kJ (418 cal); 14.4g carbohydrate; 38.8g protein; 1.3g fibre

Salads

Eggplant salad with lemon and plum dressing

4 baby eggplants (320g), cubed
3 red japanese mint (shiso) leaves, shredded finely
lemon and plum dressing
¼ cup (60ml) lemon juice
2 tablespoons pickled plum puree
2 tablespoons olive oil
2 teaspoons maple syrup
1 teaspoon salt

1 Place eggplant in large bowl, cover with cold water; stand 5 minutes.
Drain, squeezing out excess moisture.
2 Meanwhile, make lemon and plum dressing.
3 Cook eggplant in medium saucepan of boiling water about 4 minutes
or until tender; drain.
4 Divide eggplant among serving dishes; drizzle with dressing.
Sprinkle with mint.
lemon and plum dressing Whisk ingredients in a jug.

prep + cook time 15 minutes **serves** 4 as a side
nutritional count per serving 9.5g total fat (1.3g saturated fat);
585kJ (140 cal); 12g carbohydrate; 1g protein; 1.9g fibre
tips Use a combination of basil and mint leaves if you cannot find any
japanese mint (shiso).
Pickled plum puree, also known as umeboshi puree, is made from plums
(ume) slowly pickled in salt, with japanese mint (shiso) added for colour
and flavour. It is available from health food stores or Asian grocers.

Steamed chicken salad with sesame sauce

2 spring onions (50g)
2 lebanese cucumbers (260g)
250g (8 ounces) chicken thighs fillets, with skin
1 tablespoon sake
1 teaspoon sesame oil
1cm (½-inch) piece fresh ginger (5g), grated
sesame sauce
2 tablespoons sesame paste
1 tablespoon japanese soy sauce
1 tablespoon caster (superfine) sugar
1 tablespoon white sesame seeds, ground coarsely
1 teaspoon rice vinegar
1 teaspoon chilli paste
1cm (½-inch) piece fresh ginger (5g), grated
1 clove garlic, crushed

1 Chop onion finely, keeping white and green parts separate.
Halve cucumber lengthways; cut into chunks.
2 Pierce chicken with skewer; place in medium microwave-safe bowl.
Drizzle with sake and oil; sprinkle with white part of the onion and ginger.
Cook, covered, in microwave (600 Watt) 4 minutes or until cooked
through. Cool 5 minutes; reserve cooking liquid for sauce.
3 Make sesame sauce.
4 Shred chicken with hands. Place chicken in medium bowl with
cucumber and sauce; toss gently to combine. Serve, sprinkled with
green part of the onion.
sesame sauce Whisk ingredients in small bowl with 1½ tablespoons of
the reserved cooking liquid until smooth.

prep + cook time 25 minutes **serves** 4
nutritional count per serving 13.4g total fat (2.5g saturated fat);
890kJ (213 cal); 6.3g carbohydrate; 15.1g protein; 2.7g fibre
tip Traditionally, sesame paste is made by grinding toasted sesame seeds
to a rough paste in a mortar and pestle, which is available ready made.
Tahini (Greek style sesame paste) is a reasonable substitute, however it
is not made from toasted sesame so there will be a difference in flavour.

Cabbage salad

½ lebanese cucumber (65g)
1 small carrot (70g)
1 stalk celery (150g)
1 green onion (scallion)
400g (12½ ounces) wombok (napa cabbage), shredded
10g (½ ounce) shredded dried seaweed (ao-nori)
anchovy dressing
1 tablespoon sunflower oil
1 tablespoon rice wine vinegar
1 teaspoon japanese soy sauce
¼ teaspoon caster (superfine) sugar
1 anchovy fillet, chopped finely

1 Make anchovy dressing.
2 Cut cucumber, carrot, celery and onion into thin strips; place in large bowl. Add wombok and seaweed.
3 Just before serving, pour dressing over salad; toss gently to coat.
anchovy dressing Whisk ingredients in jug until sugar dissolves.

prep time 20 minutes **serves** 4
nutritional count per serving 4.9g total fat (0.5g saturated fat);
359kJ (86 cal); 4.7g carbohydrate; 2.8g protein; 6g fibre

Crab, cucumber and wakame salad

2 lebanese cucumbers (260g)
2 teaspoons salt
2 tablespoons dried seaweed (wakame)
1 cup (200g) cooked fresh crab meat
dressing
1 tablespoon rice vinegar
1 tablespoon secondary dashi (see recipe page 117)
2 teaspoons japanese soy sauce
1 teaspoon mirin
½ teaspoon fresh ginger juice

1 Make dressing.
2 Halve cucumber lengthways; discard seeds with teaspoon. Slice cucumber thinly. Place cucumber in colander. Sprinkle with salt; stand 10 minutes. Rinse under cold water; drain, gently squeezing out excess moisture. Refrigerate.
3 Meanwhile, place seaweed in small bowl, cover with cold water, stand 5 minutes; drain.
4 Arrange cucumber, seaweed and crab meat on plate; pour over dressing.
dressing Bring vinegar, dashi, sauce and mirin to the boil in small saucepan. Cool 5 minutes. Stir in juice. Refrigerate 15 minutes.

prep + cook time 20 minutes (+ refrigeration & standing) **serves** 4
nutritional count per serving 0.4g total fat (0.1g saturated fat); 176kJ (42 cal); 2g carbohydrate; 6.9g protein; 1.1g fibre
tips Try to use the freshest crab meat you can for this dish or very good quality canned crabmeat.
To obtain ginger juice, squeeze grated fresh ginger into a sieve set over a bowl. A piece of ginger measuring about 2cm (¾ inch) in length will yield 2 teaspoons of grated ginger; this amount of grated ginger should in turn yield the ½ teaspoon of juice used in this recipe.

Potato and ham salad

4 medium potatoes (500g), cut into small chunks
1 lebanese cucumber (130g)
50g (1½ ounces) sliced ham, cut into strips
mayonnaise dressing
¾ cup (185g) mayonnaise
2 tablespoons rice vinegar
½ teaspoon japanese mustard
few drops sesame oil
2 green onions (scallions), chopped finely
½ cup finely chopped fresh japanese parsley (mitsuba)

1 Boil, steam or microwave potato until tender; drain. Rinse under cold water; drain again. Place potato in medium bowl; lightly crush with back of fork (there should still be lumps).
2 Meanwhile, make mayonnaise dressing.
3 Halve cucumber lengthways; discard seeds with teaspoon. Slice cucumber thinly.
4 Add cucumber, ham and dressing to potato; toss gently to coat. Stand 15 minutes.
mayonnaise dressing Whisk mayonnaise, vinegar, mustard and oil in small bowl until smooth; stir in onion and parsley. Season to taste.

prep + cook time 45 minutes (+ standing) **serves** 4
nutritional count per serving 15.8g total fat (1.8g saturated fat); 1116kJ (267 cal); 23.9g carbohydrate; 5.4g protein; 2.6g fibre
tip Flat-leaf parsley can be substituted for mitsuba if you cannot find it.

Scallop and spinach salad

12 scallops (300g), roe removed
100g (3 ounces) baby spinach leaves
1 small red capsicum (bell pepper) (150g), cut into thin strips
¾ cup (60g) bean sprouts, trimmed
1 tablespoon black sesame seeds, toasted
lime dressing
1½ tablespoons sake
1 tablespoon lime juice
2 teaspoons shaved palm sugar
1 teaspoon fish sauce

1 Make lime dressing.
2 Cook scallop on heated oiled grill plate (or grill or barbecue).
3 Divide spinach, capsicum and sprouts among serving dishes; top with scallops. Drizzle with dressing; sprinkle with seeds.
lime dressing Whisk ingredients in small jug.

prep + cook time 15 minutes **serves** 4
nutritional count per serving 1.9g total fat (0.2g saturated fat); 263kJ (63 cal); 3.6g carbohydrate; 5.7g protein; 1.8g fibre
tip Cooking the scallops for a short time will ensure they stay moist and tender.

Coleslaw

½ small daikon (150g), cut into matchsticks
½ small wombok (napa cabbage) (350g), shredded
1 large carrot (180g), cut into matchsticks
2 spring onions (50g), sliced thinly
1 tablespoon black sesame seeds, toasted
mustard and soy dressing
½ cup (125g) mayonnaise
¼ teaspoon japanese mustard
1 ½ tablespoons rice vinegar
1 tablespoon sake
2 teaspoons japanese soy sauce
1 teaspoon caster (superfine) sugar
½ teaspoon sesame oil

1 Place daikon in colander. Sprinkle with salt; stand 15 minutes. Squeeze out excess moisture.
2 Meanwhile, make mustard and soy dressing.
3 Place daikon in large bowl with wombok, carrot, onion, seeds and dressing; toss gently to combine.
mustard and soy dressing Whisk ingredients in medium bowl until smooth.

prep time 30 minutes (+ standing) **serves** 6
nutritional count per serving 8.3g total fat (0.9g saturated fat); 531kJ (127 cal); 8.7g carbohydrate; 2g protein; 3.6g fibre

Cucumber salad

300g (9½ ounces) firm tofu
2 large green cucumbers (800g)
1 tablespoon salt
vegetable oil, for deep-frying
2 teaspoons shredded dried seaweed (wakame)
dressing
⅓ cup (80ml) mirin
¼ cup (60ml) rice vinegar
1 tablespoon japanese soy sauce
1 tablespoon primary dashi (see recipe page 116)
2 teaspoons sugar

1 Press tofu between two chopping boards with weight on top, raise one end; stand 25 minutes. Cut into cubes.

2 Halve cucumber lengthways; discard seeds with teaspoon. Slice cucumber thinly; place in colander. Sprinkle with salt; stand 30 minutes. Rinse under cold water; drain, gently squeezing out excess moisture.

3 Meanwhile, make dressing.

4 Heat oil in medium saucepan; deep-fry tofu, in batches, until golden. Drain on absorbent paper.

5 Place cucumber in medium bowl with seaweed and dressing; toss gently to combine.

6 Divide tofu among serving dishes, top with cucumber salad.

dressing Stir ingredients in small saucepan over heat, without boiling, about 5 minutes or until sugar dissolves. Cool.

prep + cook time 35 minutes (+ standing) **serves** 4
nutritional count per serving 9.7g total fat (1.3g saturated fat); 727kJ (174 cal); 4.5g carbohydrate; 10.9g protein; 6.4g fibre

Green tea noodle salad

200g (6½ ounces) green tea soba noodles, cut in half
1 tablespoon dried seaweed (wakame)
2 teaspoons vegetable oil
4 bacon slices (260g), sliced thinly
70g (2½ ounces) baby spinach leaves
150g (5½ ounces) cherry tomatoes, halved
1 avocado (250g), cut into small cubes
dressing
2 tablespoons japanese soy sauce
1 tablespoon white sesame seeds, toasted
¼ cup (60ml) rice vinegar
1½ tablespoons mirin
2½ teaspoons sesame oil
2 cloves garlic, crushed
1 teaspoon caster (superfine) sugar
1cm (½-inch) piece fresh ginger (5g), grated

1 Cook noodles in large saucepan of boiling water until tender; drain.
Rinse under cold water; drain.
2 Place seaweed in small bowl, cover with cold water, stand 5 minutes;
drain.
3 Make dressing.
4 Heat oil in large frying pan; cook bacon 5 minutes or until crispy.
Drain on absorbent paper.
5 Place noodles and two-thirds of the dressing in large bowl; toss gently
to coat. Fold through seaweed, bacon, spinach, tomatoes and avocado.
Drizzle with remaining dressing; sprinkle with extra sesame seeds,
if you like.
dressing Combine ingredients in medium bowl.

prep + cook time 25 minutes **serves** 6
nutritional count per serving 15g total fat (3.5g saturated fat);
1267kJ (303 cal); 24.8g carbohydrate; 14.4g protein; 2.7g fibre
tip Green tea soba noodles are made with buckwheat flour and
finely ground green tea, which look great when combined with bright,
fresh vegetables.

Chicken and noodle salad

500g (1 pound) chicken thigh fillets
200g (6½ ounces) snake beans, cut into chunks
300g (9½ ounces) dried udon noodles
80g (2½ ounces) baby tat soi leaves
2 cups loosely packed fresh coriander (cilantro) leaves
sesame and peanut dressing
½ cup (75g) white sesame seeds, toasted
½ cup (75g) roasted unsalted peanuts
½ cup (125ml) mirin
⅓ cup (80ml) sake

1 Place chicken in medium saucepan of boiling water; return to the boil.
Reduce heat; simmer, uncovered, about 10 minutes or until cooked
through. Cool chicken in poaching liquid 10 minutes; discard liquid.
Slice chicken thinly.
2 Meanwhile, boil, steam or microwave beans until just tender; drain.
Rinse under cold water; drain.
3 Meanwhile, make sesame and peanut dressing.
4 Cook noodles in large saucepan of boiling water until tender; drain.
Rinse under cold water; drain.
5 Place chicken, beans and noodles in large bowl with tat soi, coriander
and dressing; toss gently to combine.
sesame and peanut dressing Blend or process ingredients until smooth.

prep + cook time 30 minutes **serves** 4
nutritional count per serving 29.3g total fat (5.2g saturated fat);
2976kJ (712 cal); 55.9g carbohydrate; 43g protein; 8.1g fibre

165

Green salad

170g (5½ ounces) asparagus
8 snow peas
1 lebanese cucumber (130g)
1 small avocado (200g)
100g (3 ounces) mesclun
dressing
2 tablespoons japanese soy sauce
1½ tablespoons rice vinegar
1 tablespoon mirin
1 clove garlic, crushed
1 teaspoon caster (superfine) sugar
5mm (¼-inch) piece fresh ginger (2g), grated
2 teaspoons olive oil
½ teaspoon sesame oil

1 Make dressing.
2 Meanwhile, boil, steam or microwave asparagus and snow peas
separately until just tender; drain. Rinse under cold water; drain.
Cut into chunks.
3 Halve cucumber lengthways; discard seeds with teaspoon.
Slice cucumber thinly. Cut avocado into small cubes.
4 Place asparagus, snow peas, cucumber and avocado in large bowl
with mesclun and dressing; toss gently to combine.
dressing Place ingredients in screw-top jar; shake well. Stand 15 minutes.

prep + cook time 15 minutes **serves** 4
nutritional count per serving 10.9g total fat (2.1g saturated fat);
548kJ (131 cal); 3.5g carbohydrate; 2.9g protein; 2g fibre
tip Add some halved cherry tomatoes for colour or small Japanese rice
crackers or crispy wasabi peas for a crunch.

Somen noodle and tuna salad

100g (3 ounces) dried somen noodles
1 spring onion (25g), sliced thinly
½ lebanese cucumber (65g), sliced thinly
90g (3 ounces) can tuna in brine, drained, flaked
⅓ cup (100g) mayonnaise
¼ teaspoon light soy sauce

1 Cook noodles in medium saucepan of boiling water until tender; drain.
Rinse under cold water; drain.
2 Place onion in small bowl, cover with cold water, stand 5 minutes.
Drain squeezing out excess moisture.
3 Place cucumber in colander. Season with salt; stand 10 minutes.
Squeeze out excess moisture.
4 Place noodles, onion and cucumber in medium bowl with tuna,
mayonnaise and sauce; toss gently to combine.

prep + cook time 20 minutes (+ standing) **serves** 2
nutritional count per serving 17.9g total fat (2.3g saturated fat);
1731kJ (414 cal); 45.9g carbohydrate; 16.1g protein; 2g fibre

Five-coloured salad

6 dried shiitake mushrooms
115g (3½ ounces) green beans
120g (4 ounces) daikon
1 medium carrot (120g)
8 dried apricots, sliced thinly
1 teaspoon finely shredded lemon rind
tofu dressing
200g (6½ ounces) firm tofu
2 tablespoons tahini
1 tablespoon rice vinegar
1 tablespoon mirin
2 teaspoons sugar
2 teaspoons japanese soy sauce

1 Place mushrooms in small heatproof bowl, cover with boiling water, stand 20 minutes; drain. Discard stems; slice caps thinly.
2 Meanwhile, make tofu dressing.
3 Meanwhile, quarter beans lengthways; cut into chunks. Cut daikon and carrot into thin strips. Boil, steam or microwave beans, daikon and carrot, separately, until just tender; drain. Rinse under cold water; drain.
4 Place beans, daikon and carrot in medium bowl with apricots and dressing; toss gently to coat. Serve salad, sprinkled with rind.
tofu dressing Press tofu between two chopping boards with weight on top, raise one end; stand 25 minutes. Blend or process tofu until smooth, place in small bowl; stir in tahini. Add remaining ingredients; stir until sugar dissolves.

prep + cook time 30 minutes (+ standing) **serves** 4
nutritional count per serving 9.9g total fat (1.3g saturated fat); 765kJ (183 cal); 9.6g carbohydrate; 9.7g protein; 7.7g fibre
tip The salad and dressing can be prepared ahead and refrigerated separately. Combine just before serving.

Sesame tofu salad

2 x 300g (9½-ounce) blocks silken firm tofu
2 tablespoons sesame seeds, toasted
2 tablespoons kalonji
2 teaspoons dried chilli flakes
2 tablespoons cornflour (cornstarch)
vegetable oil, for deep-frying
100g (3 ounces) red oak lettuce leaves, torn
100g (3 ounces) mizuna
5 green onions (scallions), sliced thinly
1 large avocado (320g), chopped coarsely
1 fresh long red chilli, sliced thinly
sesame dressing
2 shallots (50g), chopped finely
2 tablespoons sesame seeds, toasted
1 tablespoon sesame oil
1 tablespoon kecap manis
1cm (½-inch) piece fresh ginger (5g), grated
¼ cup (60ml) lemon juice

1 Press tofu between two chopping boards with weight on top, raise one end; stand 25 minutes.
2 Meanwhile, make sesame dressing.
3 Cut each tofu block lengthways into four slices; dry gently with absorbent paper. Combine seeds, chilli and cornflour in large shallow bowl; press seed mixture onto both sides of tofu slices.
4 Heat oil in medium saucepan; deep-fry tofu, in batches, until golden. Remove from pan. Drain on absorbent paper.
5 Place remaining ingredients in large bowl; toss gently to combine. Divide salad among plates; top with tofu, drizzle with dressing.
sesame dressing Place ingredients in screw-top jar; shake well.

prep + cook time 35 minutes (+ standing) **serves** 4
nutritional count per serving 59.7g total fat (9.9g saturated fat); 2796kJ (699 cal); 9.2g carbohydrate; 22.8g protein; 6.2g fibre

Prawn, cucumber and wakame salad

1 lebanese cucumber (130g)
½ teaspoon salt
4 cooked medium king prawns (shrimp) (180g)
10g (½ ounce) dried seaweed (wakame)
2cm (¾-inch) piece fresh ginger (20g), sliced thinly
dressing
¼ cup (60ml) rice vinegar
1½ tablespoons primary dashi (see recipe page 116)
1½ tablespoons japanese soy sauce
1½ tablespoons mirin
3 teaspoons sugar

1 Halve cucumber lengthways; discard seeds with teaspoon. Slice
cucumber thinly; place in colander, sprinkle with salt. Stand 15 minutes.
2 Meanwhile, make dressing.
3 Rinse cucumber under cold water; drain, squeezing out excess moisture.
4 Shell and devein prawns; halve lengthways. Place in medium bowl
with 1 tablespoon of the dressing, stand 10 minutes; add cucumber.
5 Meanwhile, place seaweed in small bowl, cover with cold water,
stand 5 minutes; drain.
6 Add seaweed to prawn mixture with ginger and remaining dressing;
toss gently to combine.
dressing Stir ingredients in small saucepan; bring to the boil. Reduce
heat; simmer, stirring, until sugar dissolves. Remove from heat; cool.

prep + cook time 25 minutes (+ standing & cooling) **serves** 4
nutritional count per serving 0.4g total fat (0.1g saturated fat);
230kJ (55 cal); 4.1g carbohydrate; 6.4g protein; 1.5g fibre
tip You can substitute cooked crab meat for the prawns in this salad.

Crab and noodle salad with ginger

250g (8 ounces) dried soba noodles
¾ cup (150g) cooked crab meat, flaked
1 cup (50g) snow pea sprouts, trimmed
½ cup (40g) bean sprouts, trimmed
6 green onions (scallions), chopped finely
1½ tablespoons white sesame seeds, toasted
1 green onion (scallion), chopped finely, extra
1 tablespoon (25g) drained red pickled ginger, shredded finely
dressing
⅓ cup (80ml) vegetable oil
⅓ cup (80ml) rice vinegar
2 teaspoons japanese soy sauce
1 teaspoon sugar
½ teaspoon sesame oil

1 Cook noodles in large saucepan of boiling water until tender; drain.
Rinse noodles under cold water; drain. Chop noodles into shorter
lengths with scissors.
2 Make dressing.
3 Place noodles in large bowl with crab, sprouts, onion, dressing and
1 tablespoon of the seeds; toss gently to combine. Sprinkle salad with
remaining seeds.
4 Divide salad among serving dishes, top with extra onion and ginger.
dressing Place ingredients in screw-top jar; shake until sugar dissolves.

prep + cook time 25 minutes **serves** 4
nutritional count per serving 22.3g total fat (2.8g saturated fat);
1839kJ (440 cal); 45.2g carbohydrate; 13.3g protein; 3.1g fibre
tips You can substitute shredded chicken, sliced pressed tofu or sliced
beef for the crab.
You could use cellophane (harusame) or dried wheat (somen) noodles
instead of soba.

Tuna and soba noodle salad

270g (8½ ounces) dried soba noodles
1 lebanese cucumber (130g)
700g (1½ pounds) tuna steaks
2 green onions (scallions), sliced thinly
1 sheet toasted seaweed (yaki-nori), shredded finely
1 tablespoon black cumin seeds
coriander dressing
½ cup firmly packed fresh coriander (cilantro) leaves
¼ cup (60ml) light olive oil
¼ cup (60ml) lemon juice
2 tablespoons rice wine vinegar
1 teaspoon sesame oil
1cm (½-inch) piece fresh ginger (5g), grated
1 clove garlic, quartered

1 Cook noodles in large saucepan of boiling water until tender; drain. Rinse under cold water; drain.
2 Halve cucumber lengthways; discard seeds with teaspoon. Slice cucumber thinly.
3 Make coriander dressing.
4 Cook tuna on heated oiled grill plate (or grill or barbecue) until cooked to your liking; slice thickly.
5 Place noodles in large bowl with cucumber, onion, seaweed, seeds and dressing; toss gently to combine. Divide salad among plates; top with tuna.
coriander dressing Blend or process ingredients until smooth.

prep + cook time 30 minutes **serves** 6
nutritional count per serving 17.1g total fat (4.2g saturated fat); 1772kJ (424 cal); 31.3g carbohydrate; 34.6g protein; 1.9g fibre

Prawn and soba noodle salad

270g (8½ ounces) dried soba noodles
20 uncooked medium king prawns (shrimp) (900g)
1 medium carrot (120g), cut into matchsticks
1 small daikon (400g), cut into matchsticks
2 green onions (scallions), sliced thinly
1 fresh long red chilli, sliced thinly
½ sheet toasted seaweed (yaki-nori), shredded finely
soy dressing
2 tablespoons rice vinegar
2 tablespoons water
1 tablespoon japanese soy sauce
½ teaspoon sugar

1 Cook noodles in medium saucepan of boiling water until tender; drain. Rinse under cold water; drain.
2 Meanwhile, make soy dressing.
3 Shell and devein prawns; halve lengthways. Cook prawns in medium saucepan of boiling water, uncovered, until changed in colour. Drain; cool.
4 Place noodles, prawns and dressing in large bowl with carrot, daikon, onion and chilli. Serve salad sprinkled with seaweed.
soy dressing Place ingredients in screw-top jar; shake well.

prep + cook time 20 minutes **serves** 6
nutritional count per serving 1.1g total fat (0.2g saturated fat); 1003kJ (240 cal); 33.8g carbohydrate; 21.3g protein; 3.1g fibre

181

Soba and daikon salad

300g (9½ ounces) dried soba noodles
1 small daikon (400g), cut into matchsticks
4 green onions (scallions), sliced thinly
1 teaspoon sesame oil
100g (3 ounces) enoki mushrooms
2 tablespoons (46g) drained pink pickled ginger, sliced thinly
1 sheet toasted seaweed (yaki-nori), sliced thinly
mirin and sake dressing
¼ cup (60ml) mirin
2 tablespoons kecap manis
1 tablespoon sake
1 clove garlic, crushed
1cm (½-inch) piece fresh ginger (5g), grated
1 teaspoon sugar

1 Cook noodles in large saucepan of boiling water until tender; drain.
Rinse under cold water; drain.
2 Make mirin and sake dressing.
3 Place noodles in large bowl with daikon, onion and half the dressing;
toss gently to combine.
4 Heat oil in small frying pan; cook mushrooms, stirring, 2 minutes.
5 Divide salad among serving dishes; top with combined mushrooms,
ginger and seaweed. Drizzle with remaining dressing.
mirin and sake dressing Place ingredients in screw-top jar; shake well.

prep + cook time 35 minutes **serves** 4
nutritional count per serving 2.4g total fat (0.3g saturated fat);
1292kJ (309 cal); 56.6g carbohydrate; 10.9g protein; 5.3g fibre

Daikon and carrot salad

2 medium carrots (240g), cut into matchsticks
360g (11½ ounces) daikon, cut into matchsticks
4 japanese mint (shiso) leaves
1 tablespoon finely shredded lemon rind
1 teaspoon black sesame seeds, toasted
⅓ cup (80ml) sushi vinegar (see recipe page 98)

1 Place carrot and daikon in separate medium bowls, cover with iced water, stand 15 minutes; drain, gently squeezing out excess moisture.
2 Place mint leaves on top of each other and roll up; cut into thin strips.
3 Place carrot, daikon and mint in medium bowl; toss gently to combine. Serve sprinkled with rind and seeds, drizzled with vinegar.

prep time 15 minutes (+ standing) **serves** 4
nutritional count per serving 0.7g total fat (0g saturated fat); 167kJ (40 cal); 5.1g carbohydrate; 1.1g protein; 3.1g fibre
tip This refreshing salad is a perfect accompaniment to barbecued meat or fish.

Sushi salad

2 cups (400g) japanese rice (koshihikari)
2 cups (500ml) water
2 lebanese cucumbers (260g)
½ small daikon (200g)
1 medium lemon (140g), unpeeled, quartered, sliced thinly
400g (12½-ounce) piece sashimi salmon, sliced thinly
¼ cup (35g) white sesame seeds, toasted
1 sheet toasted seaweed (yaki-nori), shredded finely
mirin and wasabi dressing
4cm (1½-inch) piece fresh ginger (20g), grated
2 tablespoons mirin
1 teaspoon wasabi paste
1 tablespoon light soy sauce
⅓ cup (80ml) water
¼ cup (60ml) rice wine vinegar

1 Rinse rice in strainer under cold water until water runs clear. Place drained rice and the water in medium saucepan, cover tightly; bring to the boil. Reduce heat; simmer, covered tightly, about 12 minutes or until water is absorbed and rice is just cooked. Remove from heat; stand rice, covered, 10 minutes.
2 Meanwhile, make mirin and wasabi dressing.
3 Using vegetable peeler, slice cucumber into ribbons. Slice daikon thinly; cut slices into matchsticks.
4 Place rice, cucumber and daikon in large bowl with lemon, salmon, dressing and half the seeds; toss gently to combine.
5 Divide salad among bowls; top with seaweed and remaining seeds.
mirin and wasabi dressing Place ingredients in screw-top jar; shake well.

prep + cook time 40 minutes **serves** 4
nutritional count per serving 12.7g total fat (2.3g saturated fat); 2445kJ (585 cal); 83g carbohydrate; 29.3g protein; 5.7g fibre

Millet and tofu salad

1 cup (200g) millet
2 fresh long red chillies, chopped finely
⅓ cup (45g) roasted unsalted coarsely chopped peanuts
400g (12½ ounces) firm marinated tofu, cut into batons
100g (3 ounces) snow peas, trimmed, sliced lengthways
230g (7 ounces) can bamboo shoots, rinsed, drained, sliced thinly
½ small red onion (50g), sliced thinly
mirin dressing
¼ cup (60ml) mirin
1 tablespoon japanese soy sauce
1 tablespoon rice vinegar
1 clove garlic, crushed

1 Cook millet in medium saucepan of boiling water, uncovered, until just tender; drain. Cool.
2 Meanwhile, make mirin dressing.
3 Combine millet in large bowl with chilli, nuts and half the dressing.
4 Combine remaining ingredients and remaining dressing in medium bowl.
5 Serve millet mixture topped with tofu salad.
mirin dressing Place ingredients in screw-top jar; shake well.

prep + cook time 35 minutes **serves** 4
nutritional count per serving 14.4g total fat (2.2g saturated fat); 1676kJ (401 cal); 39.3g carbohydrate; 22g protein; 8.8g fibre
tip We used cryovac-packed ready-to-serve sweet chilli tofu, available from many supermarkets and Asian food stores.

Smoked salmon, avocado and udon salad

250g (8 ounces) dried udon noodles
300g (9½ ounces) sliced smoked salmon
90g (3 ounces) snow pea sprouts, trimmed
2 tablespoons finely chopped fresh chives
1 small red onion (100g), chopped finely
2 small avocados (450g), diced
lime and wasabi dressing
⅓ cup (80ml) light olive oil
2 tablespoons rice vinegar
1 tablespoon mirin
1 tablespoon lime juice
2 teaspoons wasabi paste

1 Cook noodles in large saucepan of boiling water until tender; drain.
Rinse under cold water; drain.
2 Meanwhile, make lime and wasabi dressing.
3 Separate smoked salmon slices; cut into small strips.
4 Just before serving, place noodles and salmon in large bowl with
sprouts, chives, onion, avocado and dressing; toss gently to combine.
lime and wasabi dressing Place ingredients in screw-top jar; shake well.

prep + cook time 25 minutes **serves** 4
nutritional count per serving 40.6g total fat (7.4g saturated fat);
2888kJ (691 cal); 50.2g carbohydrate; 28.2g protein; 4.7g fibre

Omelette salad

1 medium daikon (600g)
2 medium carrots (240g)
6 large red radishes (210g), sliced thinly
120g (4 ounces) red cabbage, shredded finely
1½ cups (120g) bean sprouts, trimmed
2 tablespoons (46g) drained pink pickled ginger, sliced thinly
6 green onions (scallions), sliced thinly
4 eggs
1 tablespoon japanese soy sauce
½ sheet toasted seaweed (yaki-nori), sliced thinly
wasabi dressing
2 tablespoons japanese soy sauce
1 tablespoon pink pickled ginger juice
1 tablespoon mirin
1 teaspoon wasabi paste

1 Make wasabi dressing.
2 Using vegetable peeler, slice daikon and carrot into thin strips. Place in large bowl with radish, cabbage, sprouts, ginger and three-quarters of the onion.
3 Combine egg, sauce and seaweed in small jug. Pour half of the egg mixture in large heated oiled frying pan; cook, uncovered, until just set. Slide omelette onto plate; roll into cigar shape. Slice omelette roll into thin rings. Repeat with remaining egg mixture.
4 Pour dressing over salad; toss gently to combine. Divide salad among serving dishes; top with omelette rings and remaining onion.
wasabi dressing Place ingredients in screw-top jar; shake well.

prep + cook time 25 minutes **serves** 4
nutritional count per serving 6.8g total fat (1.9g saturated fat); 744kJ (178 cal); 13.4g carbohydrate; 11.9g protein; 6.8g fibre

Seafood

Seafood and udon noodle stir-fry

10 uncooked medium king prawns (shrimp) (450g)
400g (12½ ounces) dried udon noodles
2 tablespoons sunflower oil
4 small cleaned squid hoods (300g), cut into rings
100g (3 ounces) fresh shiitake mushrooms, sliced thinly
4 green onions (scallions), chopped coarsely
1 tablespoon shredded dried seaweed (ao-nori)
2½ cups (200g) bean sprouts, trimmed
⅓ cup bonito flakes
⅓ cup (80ml) japanese soy sauce

1 Shell and devein prawns.
2 Cook noodles in large saucepan of boiling water until tender; drain. Rinse; drain.
3 Heat oil in wok; stir-fry squid and prawns 2 minutes. Add mushrooms, onion, seaweed and half the sprouts; stir-fry 2 minutes. Add noodles and remaining ingredients to wok; stir-fry until hot. Serve topped with remaining sprouts

prep + cook time 25 minutes **serves** 4
nutritional count per serving 11.7g total fat (1.5g saturated fat); 2332kJ (558 cal); 70.1g carbohydrate; 38.9g protein; 5.7g fibre

Tuna tartare on rice

1 cup (200g) japanese rice (koshihikari)
150g (5½-ounce) piece sashimi tuna, chopped finely
2 green onions (scallions), chopped finely
10 japanese mint (shiso) leaves, chopped finely
2cm (¾-inch) piece fresh ginger (10g), grated
2 cups (500ml) water
50g (1½ ounces) daikon, cut into matchsticks
4 egg yolks
1 tablespoon (15g) salmon roe

1 Place rice in large bowl, cover with cold water. Stir; drain. Repeat process two or three times until water is almost clear. Drain in strainer; stand 10 minutes.
2 Meanwhile, combine tuna, onion, mint and ginger in medium bowl.
3 Place rice and the water in medium saucepan, cover tightly; bring to the boil. Reduce heat; simmer, covered tightly, on low heat about 12 minutes or until water is absorbed. Remove from heat; stand rice, covered, 5 minutes.
4 To serve, divide hot rice among serving bowls; top with daikon and tuna mixture. Make small well in centre, position egg yolk in well. Top with roe and serve immediately with japanese soy sauce, if you like.

prep + cook time 30 minutes **serves** 4
nutritional count per serving 6.1g total fat (1.7g saturated fat); 1187kJ (284 cal); 40g carbohydrate; 16.6g protein; 0.6g fibre
tip Use a combination of basil and mint leaves if you cannot find any japanese mint (shiso).

Grilled sardines

250g (8 ounces) green beans
80g (2½ ounces) snow peas, trimmed
20 sardine fillets (600g)
1 tablespoon sesame oil
1 tablespoon sunflower oil
1 clove garlic, sliced thinly
2 teaspoons japanese soy sauce

1 Boil, steam or microwave beans and peas separately until just tender; drain. Rinse under cold water; drain. Halve beans and peas lengthways.
2 Cook sardines, skin-side down, on heated oiled grill plate (or grill or barbecue) 5 minutes or until skin is crisp.
3 Meanwhile, heat oils in medium frying pan; cook garlic until fragrant. Add beans and peas; cook, stirring, until tender.
4 Divide bean and pea mixture among serving plates; top with sardines, drizzle over sauce.

prep + cook time 15 minutes **serves** 4
nutritional count per serving 18.4g total fat (3.3g saturated fat); 1087kJ (260 cal); 2.6g carbohydrate; 20.4g protein; 2.3g fibre
tip If using a grill (broiler), place sardines skin-side up on oiled oven tray.

Seafood hotpot

12 medium black mussels (300g)
12 uncooked medium king prawns (shrimp) (540g)
12 scallops (300g), without roe
400g (12½ ounces) firm white fish fillets, cut into cubes
⅓ cup (80ml) japanese soy sauce
⅓ cup (80ml) sake
2 teaspoons mirin
1 tablespoon vegetable oil
2 cloves garlic, crushed
5cm (2-inch) piece fresh ginger (25g), chopped finely
3 cups (750ml) fish stock
1 cup (250ml) water
1 teaspoon powdered dashi
1 small kumara (orange sweet potato) (250g),
　halved lengthways, sliced thinly
250g (8 ounces) spinach, chopped coarsely
2 green onions (scallions), chopped coarsely
270g (8½ ounces) dried udon noodles

1 Scrub mussels; remove beards. Shell and devein prawns, leaving tails intact.
2 Combine mussels, prawns, scallops, fish, 1 tablespoon each of sauce and sake, and mirin in large bowl.
3 Heat oil in large saucepan; cook garlic and ginger, stirring, until fragrant. Add stock, the water, dashi and remaining sauce and sake; bring to the boil. Add kumara; cook, uncovered, 2 minutes. Add undrained seafood; cook, covered, about 5 minutes or until mussels open (discard any that do not). Add spinach and onion; cook, uncovered, until spinach wilts.
4 Meanwhile, cook noodles in large saucepan of boiling water until tender; drain.
5 Divide noodles among serving bowls; top with seafood mixture.

prep + cook time 40 minutes **serves** 4
nutritional count per serving 7.8g total fat (1.3g saturated fat); 2307kJ (552 cal); 57.3g carbohydrate; 56.8g protein; 4.5g fibre

'Tatsuta age' snapper

2 snapper fillets (500g)
2 tablespoons sake
2 tablespoons japanese soy sauce
1 tablespoon mirin
2cm (¾-inch) piece fresh ginger (10g), grated
¾ cup (75g) potato starch
vegetable oil, for deep-frying
1 green onion (scallion), sliced thinly
2 medium lemons (280g), cut into wedges

1 Check fish for bones; cut into 4cm (1½-inch) cubes.
2 Combine fish, sake, sauce, mirin and ginger in medium bowl; stand 20 minutes.
3 Drain fish; discard marinade. Toss fish in potato starch; shake off excess.
4 Heat oil in saucepan; deep-fry fish until crisp and golden. Sprinkle with onion; serve with lemon wedges.

prep + cook time 30 minutes (+ standing) **serves** 4
nutritional count per serving 11.5g total fat (1.9g saturated fat); 1204kJ (288 cal); 15.2g carbohydrate; 26.2g protein; 2.1g fibre
tip Serve snapper with a tempura dipping sauce for extra flavour (see recipe page 15).

Grilled tuna with chilled soba salad

250g (8 ounces) dried soba noodles
¼ cup (70g) drained pickled pink ginger, sliced thinly
4 green onions (scallions), sliced thinly
4 tuna steaks (700g)
1 sheet toasted seaweed (yaki-nori), shredded
soy mirin dressing
¼ cup (60ml) light soy sauce
⅓ cup (80ml) mirin
2 tablespoons sake
1 tablespoon rice vinegar
1 teaspoon sesame oil
1 teaspoon wasabi paste

1 Cook noodles in large saucepan of boiling water until tender; drain. Rinse under cold water; drain.
2 Make soy mirin dressing.
3 Place cold noodles in large bowl with ginger, onion and three-quarters of the dressing; toss gently to combine. Cover; refrigerate until chilled.
4 Cook tuna on heated oiled grill plate (or grill or barbecue) until just cooked (do not overcook tuna or it will dry out).
5 Divide noodle salad among serving dishes; top with tuna, drizzle with remaining dressing and sprinkle with seaweed.
soy mirin dressing Place ingredients in screw-top jar; shake well.

prep + cook time 30 minutes (+ refrigeration) **serves** 4
nutritional count per serving 11.9g total fat (4.3g saturated fat); 2207kJ (528 cal); 45.1g carbohydrate; 52.1g protein; 2.8g fibre

Free-form sushi

1 cup (200g) japanese rice (koshihikari)
2 cups (500ml) water
1 cup (250ml) japanese soy sauce
1½ teaspoons caster (superfine) sugar
1 small carrot (70g), cut into short matchsticks
1 small zucchini (90g), sliced thinly
6 cooked small king prawns (shrimp) (150g)
200g (6½ ounces) sliced smoked salmon, sliced thinly
200g (6½-ounce) piece sashimi tuna, diced
120g (4-ounce) piece sashimi white fish, diced
1 thick omelette (see recipe page 61), diced
50g (1½ ounces) salmon roe
¼ cup finely chopped fresh chives

1 Place rice in large bowl, cover with cold water. Stir; drain. Repeat process two or three times until water is almost clear. Drain rice in strainer; stand 10 minutes. Place rice and the water in medium saucepan, cover tightly; bring to the boil. Reduce heat; simmer, covered tightly, on low heat about 12 minutes or until water is absorbed. Remove from heat; stand rice, covered, 5 minutes. Cut through rice with wooden spoon to separate grains. Cool, covered with clean tea towel.
2 Stir sauce and sugar in medium saucepan over heat until sugar dissolves. Add carrot and zucchini; cook until carrot softens. Remove from heat. Strain carrots and zucchini into small bowl; reserve sauce. Cool.
3 Just before serving, spread rice onto large platter. Sprinkle over seafood, omelette and vegetables. Top with roe; sprinkle with chives. Serve with reserved sauce for dipping and pickled ginger, if you like.

prep + cook time 55 minutes (+ standing) **serves** 8
nutritional count per serving 4.2g total fat (1g saturated fat); 970kJ (232 cal); 22.1g carbohydrate; 25.2g protein; 0.6g fibre
tip For the white fish you can try either kingfish or snapper.

Sake-glazed salmon

1 tablespoon vegetable oil
1 teaspoon sesame oil
4 salmon fillets (700g)
40g (1½ ounces) butter
¼ cup (60ml) sake
1½ tablespoons japanese soy sauce
1 tablespoon mirin
2 teaspoons caster (superfine) sugar
5mm (¼-inch) piece fresh ginger (2g), grated

1 Heat oils in large frying pan; cook salmon, skin-side down, 3 minutes or until skin is golden. Turn fillet; cook 2-3 minutes or until rare. Remove from pan; cover to keep warm.
2 Discard oil from pan. Add butter, sake, sauce, mirin, sugar and ginger; stir until sugar dissolves. Bring to the boil; cook, stirring, about 2 minutes or until sauce thickens slightly.
3 Serve salmon drizzled with glaze.

prep + cook time 20 minutes **serves** 4
nutritional count per serving 26.4g total fat (8.9g saturated fat); 1659kJ (397 cal); 2.6g carbohydrate; 34.7g protein; 0g fibre
tips Check the salmon for bones, pulling out any with clean tweezers. Serve salmon with steamed rice and a simple green salad.

Sesame tuna steaks with nori rice

1 cup (200g) japanese rice (koshihikari)
2 cups (500ml) water
4 tuna steaks (600g)
¾ cup (115g) white sesame seeds
½ cup (125g) mayonnaise
3 teaspoons wasabi paste
2½ tablespoons rice wine vinegar
1 tablespoon mirin
1 teaspoon sugar
¼ teaspoon salt
1 sheet toasted seaweed (yaki-nori), shredded
¼ cup (60ml) peanut oil

1 Place rice in large bowl, cover with cold water. Stir; drain. Repeat process two or three times until water is almost clear. Drain rice in strainer; stand 10 minutes. Place rice and the water in medium saucepan, cover tightly; bring to the boil. Reduce heat; simmer, covered tightly, on low heat about 12 minutes or until water is absorbed. Remove from heat; stand rice, covered, 5 minutes.
2 Meanwhile, coat tuna in seeds, pressing down to coat well. Refrigerate.
3 Combine mayonnaise and wasabi in small bowl.
4 Combine vinegar, mirin, sugar and salt in small bowl; pour over hot rice, cutting through with fork to separate grains. Fold in seaweed; keep warm.
5 Heat oil in large frying pan; cook steaks 1-2 minutes each side or until seeds are crisp and golden (tuna should still be pink in the middle). Drain on absorbent paper.
6 Serve tuna with rice and wasabi mayonnaise.

prep + cook time 35 minutes **serves** 4
nutritional count per serving 48.9g total fat (9.3g saturated fat); 3474kJ (831 cal); 47.7g carbohydrate; 47.8g protein; 3.6g fibre
tips The crunchy sesame seed crust on the tuna gives a nutty aroma while leaving the tuna rare.
Cut the nori sheets lengthways into six strips using scissors, then overlap the strips and cut widthways into fine flakes.

Salt and pepper salmon with wasabi mayonnaise

2 teaspoons sea salt
2 teaspoons japanese pepper
1 ½ tablespoons vegetable oil
4 salmon fillets (800g), skin on
½ cup (150g) mayonnaise
2 teaspoons wasabi paste
1 teaspoon finely chopped fresh coriander (cilantro)
1 teaspoon lime juice

1 Blend, process or grind salt and pepper until fine. Combine pepper mixture, oil and fish in large bowl; stand 5 minutes.
2 Meanwhile, combine mayonnaise, wasabi, coriander and juice in small bowl.
3 Cook fish on heated oiled grill plate (or grill or barbecue) until cooked to your liking.
4 Serve salmon with wasabi mayonnaise, and watercress, if you like.

prep + cook time 25 minutes **serves** 4
nutritional count per serving 40.1g total fat (6.3g saturated fat); 2278kJ (545 cal); 7.5g carbohydrate; 39.4 protein; 0.2g fibre

Steamed snapper with wakame

2 tablespoons dried seaweed (wakame)
4 snapper fillets (700g)
2 tablespoons sake
2 green onions (scallions), sliced thinly
20g (¾ ounce) butter
ginger and lemon dipping sauce
2cm (¾-inch) piece fresh ginger (10g), grated
1 tablespoon lemon juice
2 teaspoons japanese soy sauce
¼ teaspoon sesame oil

1 Place seaweed in small bowl, cover with cold water, stand 5 minutes; drain.
2 Place each fillet on a square of oiled baking (parchment) paper or foil large enough to completely enclose fish; top each fillet with sake, seaweed, onion and butter. Gather corners of paper squares together above fish; twist to enclose securely.
3 Place parcels in large bamboo steamer. Steam, covered, over wok or large frying pan of simmering water about 10 minutes or until fish is cooked through.
4 Meanwhile, make ginger and lemon dipping sauce.
5 Serve fish with dipping sauce.
ginger and lemon dipping sauce Combine ingredients in small bowl.

prep + cook time 20 minutes (+ standing) **serves** 4
nutritional count per serving 7.2g total fat (3.8g saturated fat); 924kJ (221 cal); 0.6g carbohydrate; 36g protein; 0.5g fibre

Tuna and potato salad

300g (9½ ounces) snow peas
6 kipfler (fingerling) potatoes (500g), sliced thickly
150g (5½ ounces) cherry tomatoes, halved
2 green onions (scallions), sliced thinly
¼ cup (40g) kalamata olives
¼ cup loosely packed fresh flat-leaf parsley leaves
1 tablespoon vegetable oil
4 tuna fillets (700g)
lemon and soy dressing
¼ cup (60ml) extra virgin olive oil
2 tablespoons rice vinegar
1½ tablespoons lemon juice
2 teaspoons japanese soy sauce
½ teaspoon sesame oil
¼ teaspoon japanese mustard
1 clove garlic, crushed

1 Boil, steam or microwave peas until just tender; drain. Rinse under cold water; drain. Halve crossways on the diagonal.
2 Boil, steam or microwave potato until tender; drain. Rinse under cold water; drain. Halve lengthways.
3 Meanwhile, make lemon and soy dressing.
4 Place peas and potatoes in medium bowl with tomatoes, onion, olives, parsley and dressing; toss gently to combine.
5 Heat oil in large frying pan; cook fillets about 2 minutes each side or until rare.
6 Divide tuna and salad among serving dishes.
lemon and soy dressing Whisk ingredients in jug until smooth.

prep + cook time 30 minutes **serves** 4
nutritional count per serving 30.8g total fat (6.8g saturated fat); 2412kJ (577 cal); 21.5g carbohydrate; 49.9g protein; 5.5g fibre

Seafood doria

1 tablespoon olive oil
20g (¾ ounce) butter
1 medium onion (150g), chopped
3 rindless bacon slices (195g),
  chopped
1 medium red capsicum (bell
  pepper) (200g), diced finely
150g (5½ ounces) shimeji
  mushrooms, pulled apart
1 clove garlic, crushed
20 uncooked small king prawns
  (shrimp) (500g), peeled, deveined
600g (1¼ pounds) firm white
  fish fillets, diced
¼ cup (60g) tomato paste
2 tablespoons mirin
¼ teaspoon dashi granules

1 cup (250ml) water
7 cups cooked japanese rice
  (koshihikari)
1 sheet toasted seaweed
  (yaki-nori), shredded
1 cup (75g) japanese breadcrumbs
¾ cup (75g) grated mozzarella
  cheese
½ cup (50g) grated parmesan
  cheese
béchamel sauce
50g (1½ ounces) butter
⅓ cup (50g) plain (all-purpose) flour
large pinch freshly grated nutmeg
2⅓ cups (580ml) milk
1 bay leaf
½ cup (125ml) pouring cream

1 Preheat oven to 200°C/400°F. Oil eight 1½-cup (375ml) ovenproof dishes.
2 Make béchamel sauce.
3 Heat half the oil and half the butter in deep frying pan; cook onion,
stirring, 5 minutes or until softened. Add bacon, capsicum, mushrooms
and garlic; cook 7 minutes or until vegetables soften. Remove from pan.
4 Add remaining oil and butter to same pan; cook prawns until pink.
Remove from pan. Cook fish in same pan, stirring, 2 minutes or until
flesh turns opaque. Remove from pan. Add tomato paste, mirin, dashi
granules and the water to pan, scraping any brown bits from base of pan.
Bring to the boil; remove from heat.
5 Return vegetables and seafood to pan with rice and seaweed; combine.
Spoon rice mixture into dish; top with béchamel. Sprinkle with combined
breadcrumbs and cheeses. Bake 45 minutes or until golden and bubbling.
béchamel sauce Melt butter in medium saucepan. Add flour and nutmeg;
cook, stirring, until mixture bubbles and thickens. Whisk in milk; add leaf, stir
until mixture thickens. Remove from heat; stir in cream, cool. Discard leaf.

prep + cook time 2 hours 15 minutes **serves** 8
nutritional count per serving 27.5g total fat (15.4g saturated fat);
2897kJ (693 cal); 67.3g carbohydrate; 41.9g protein; 2.5g fibre
tip You need to cook 2½ cups (500g) of japanese rice for this recipe.

Salmon teriyaki

120g (4 ounces) daikon, shredded finely
4 salmon fillets (700g), skinned
teriyaki marinade
⅔ cup (160ml) japanese soy sauce
⅔ cup (160ml) mirin
2 tablespoons sake
1 tablespoon sugar

1 Place daikon in small bowl, cover with iced water, stand 15 minutes; drain.
2 Meanwhile, make teriyaki marinade.
3 Combine salmon and marinade in medium bowl; stand 10 minutes, turning occasionally.
4 Drain salmon over medium bowl; reserve marinade. Cook salmon on heated oiled grill plate (or grill or barbecue), brushing occasionally with marinade, until cooked as you like.
5 Bring reserved marinade to the boil in small saucepan. Reduce heat; simmer 5 minutes or until sauce thickens slightly.
6 Serve salmon with daikon; drizzle with sauce.
teriyaki marinade Stir ingredients in medium bowl until sugar dissolves.

prep + cook time 20 minutes (+ standing) **serves** 4
nutritional count per serving 12.5g total fat (2.8g saturated fat); 1333kJ (319 cal); 7.2g carbohydrate; 36.7g protein; 0.5g fibre
tip Ready-made teriyaki sauce may be used, but it's stronger than homemade. Dilute it with a little mirin, sake or water, according to taste.

Seafood tempura

12 uncooked medium king prawns (shrimp) (540g)
2 small cleaned squid hoods (150g)
2 medium brown onions (300g)
8 fresh shiitake mushrooms or large button mushrooms
2 sheets toasted seaweed (yaki-nori)
20g (½ ounce) dried somen noodles, cut in half

vegetable oil, for deep-frying
12 scallops (300g), roe removed
300g (12½ ounces) thin white fish fillets, cut into cubes
1 small red capsicum (bell pepper) (150g), cut into squares
plain (all-purpose) flour, for dusting
1 quantity tempura batter (see recipe page 332)
1 medium lemon (140g), cut into wedges

1 Shell and devein prawns, leaving tails intact. Make three small cuts on underside of each prawn, halfway through flesh, to prevent curling when cooked. Trim a thin edge off each tail and, with the back of a knife, gently press to expel any moisture that might make the oil spit during cooking.
2 Cut squid down centre to open out; score inside in diagonal pattern then cut into large squares or strips.
3 Halve onions from root end. Insert toothpicks at regular intervals to hold onion rings together and slice in between. Discard mushroom stems; cut a cross in top of caps.
4 Cut one sheet seaweed into 5cm (2-inch) squares; halve the other sheet and cut into 2cm (¾-inch) wide strips. Brush seaweed strips with water and wrap tightly around middle of about 10 noodles; reserve noodle bunches.
5 Heat oil in large saucepan. Dust seafood and vegetables, except seaweed squares, lightly in flour; shake off excess flour. Dip seaweed squares and other ingredients in batter, drain excess; deep-fry ingredients, in batches, until golden. Drain on absorbent paper. Only fry small amounts at a time and make sure enough time is allowed for oil to come back to correct temperature before adding next batch.
6 Deep-fry reserved noodle bundles and serve as garnish. Serve with lemon wedges and warm tempura dipping sauce (see recipe page 15).

prep + cook time 40 minutes **serves** 4
nutritional count per serving 29.9g total fat (4.2g saturated fat); 3081kJ (737 cal); 67.9g carbohydrate; 45.9g protein; 4.5g fibre

Tuna skewers

800g (1½ pounds) tuna steaks, cubed
2 tablespoons olive oil
3 teaspoons wasabi paste
1 teaspoon ground coriander
⅓ cup finely chopped fresh coriander (cilantro)
300g (9½ ounces) dried soba noodles
1 medium carrot (120g), cut into matchsticks
4 green onions (scallions), sliced thickly
¼ cup firmly packed fresh coriander (cilantro) leaves
mirin and ginger dressing
¼ cup (60ml) mirin
2 tablespoons japanese soy sauce
1cm (½-inch) piece fresh ginger (5g), grated
1 teaspoon sesame oil
1 teaspoon fish sauce
1 teaspoon sugar

1 Combine tuna, oil, wasabi and ground coriander in large bowl. Thread tuna onto eight skewers; sprinkle with chopped coriander.
2 Cook noodles in large saucepan of boiling water until tender; drain. Rinse under cold water; drain.
3 Meanwhile, make mirin and ginger dressing.
4 Place noodles in large bowl with carrot, onion, coriander leaves and half the dressing; toss gently to combine.
5 Cook skewers on heated oiled grill plate (or grill or barbecue) until cooked as you like (do not overcook or tuna will dry out).
6 Serve skewers on noodles, drizzled with remaining dressing.
mirin and ginger dressing Place ingredients in screw-top jar; shake well.

prep + cook time 30 minutes **serves** 4
nutritional count per serving 22.5g total fat (6.2g saturated fat); 2847kJ (681 cal); 55g carbohydrate; 59.9g protein; 3.7g fibre
tip You will need to soak eight bamboo skewers in water for at least an hour to prevent them from splintering and scorching.

227

Calamari teppanyaki

1 ½ cups (300g) japanese rice (koshihikari)
3 cups (750ml) water
1kg (2 pounds) calamari rings
1 tablespoon peanut oil
4 fresh small red thai chillies (serrano chilies), chopped finely
1 teaspoon finely grated lemon rind
1 clove garlic, crushed
2 tablespoons (46g) drained pickled pink ginger, sliced thinly
6 green onions (scallions), sliced thickly
2 lebanese cucumbers (260g), seeded, chopped finely
lemon soy dipping sauce
¼ cup (60ml) rice vinegar
1 tablespoon sugar
1 tablespoon japanese soy sauce
1 teaspoon finely grated lemon rind

1 Make lemon soy dipping sauce.
2 Place rice in large bowl, cover with cold water. Stir; drain. Repeat process two or three times until water is almost clear. Drain rice in strainer; stand 10 minutes. Place rice and the water in medium saucepan, cover tightly; bring to the boil. Reduce heat; simmer, covered tightly, on low heat about 12 minutes or until water is absorbed. Remove from heat; stand rice, covered, 5 minutes.
3 Meanwhile, combine calamari, oil, quarter of the chilli, rind and garlic in large bowl. Cook calamari on heated oiled flat plate (or grill or barbecue) until tender.
4 Divide rice and calamari among plates with ginger, onion, cucumber and remaining chilli; serve with dipping sauce.
lemon soy dipping sauce Stir vinegar, sugar and sauce in small saucepan over heat until sugar dissolves. Remove from heat; stir in rind.

prep + cook time 30 minutes **serves** 4
nutritional count per serving 8.1g total fat (1.9g saturated fat); 2240kJ (536 cal); 65.9g carbohydrate; 47.6g protein; 2g fibre

Whiting tempura

¼ cup (60ml) japanese soy sauce
2 tablespoons sweet chilli sauce
2 tablespoons room temperature water
1 tablespoon lemon juice
2 green onions (scallions), sliced thinly
1 egg
¾ cup (180ml) iced water
½ cup (75g) plain (all-purpose) flour
½ cup (75g) cornflour (cornstarch)
vegetable oil, for deep-frying
12 whiting fillets (840g)

1 Combine sauces, the room temperature water, juice and onion in small bowl.
2 Whisk egg and the iced water in medium bowl; stir in sifted flours all at once. Do not overmix; batter should be lumpy.
3 Heat oil in large saucepan. Dip fillets, one at a time, in batter; deep-fry, in batches, until browned lightly and just cooked through. Drain on absorbent paper. Serve with dipping sauce.

prep + cook time 25 minutes **serves** 4
nutritional count per serving 20.6g total fat (3.1g saturated fat); 2107kJ (504 cal); 31.8g carbohydrate; 46.5g protein; 1.3g fibre
tips If serving whiting tempura as finger food, cut fish fillets into bite-sized pieces before coating in batter.
Place fried fish in slow oven to keep warm while cooking remaining batches.

Ginger tuna with wasabi cream

4 tuna steaks (800g)
½ cup (125ml) olive oil
2cm (¾-inch) piece fresh ginger (10g), grated
3 fresh red thai chillies (serrano chilies), seeded, chopped finely
10cm (4-inch) stick fresh lemon grass (20g), chopped finely
wasabi cream
1 cup (250ml) white wine
2 tablespoons finely chopped palm sugar
⅓ cup (80ml) cider vinegar
1 tablespoon wasabi paste
300g (9½ ounces) crème fraîche

1 Combine tuna, oil, ginger, chilli and lemon grass in large bowl. Cover; refrigerate 3 hours or overnight.
2 Make wasabi cream.
3 Drain tuna; reserve marinade. Cook tuna on heated oiled grill plate (or grill or barbecue), brushing with reserved marinade, until browned both sides and just cooked through.
4 Serve tuna with wasabi cream.
wasabi cream Stir wine, sugar and vinegar in small saucepan over low heat; simmer, uncovered, until reduced by half. Cool slightly. Stir in paste and crème fraîche.

prep + cook time 20 minutes (+ refrigeration) **serves** 4
nutritional count per serving 70.4g total fat (28.7g saturated fat); 3837kJ (918 cal); 9.6g carbohydrate; 52.4g protein; 0.3g fibre
tip Wasabi cream can be made ahead. Cover; refrigerate overnight.

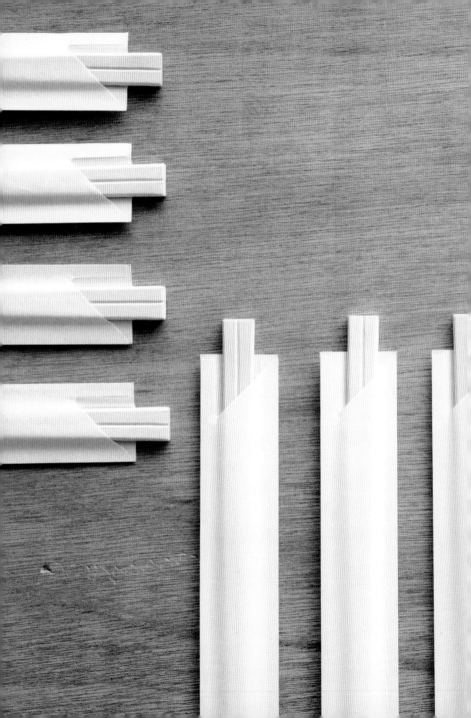

Poultry

Chicken and vegetable skewers

4 fresh shiitake mushrooms
500g (1 pound) chicken thigh fillets, cut into chunks
1 medium red capsicum (bell pepper) (200g), chopped coarsely
6 thick green onions (scallions), cut into chunks
¼ teaspoon japanese pepper
sauce
½ cup (125ml) japanese soy sauce
½ cup (125ml) sake
¼ cup (60ml) mirin
2 tablespoons sugar

1 Make sauce.
2 Meanwhile, discard mushroom stems; halve caps. Thread chicken and vegetables onto eight bamboo skewers, leaving space between pieces to allow even cooking.
3 Cook skewers, in batches, on heated oiled grill plate (or grill or barbecue), turning and brushing with sauce occasionally, until browned all over and cooked through. Serve sprinkled with pepper.
sauce Bring ingredients to the boil in small saucepan. Reduce heat; simmer, uncovered, over medium heat until sauce reduces by a third. Cool.

prep + cook time 35 minutes (+ cooling) **serves** 4
nutritional count per serving 9.1g total fat (2.8g saturated fat); 1108kJ (265 cal); 11.9g carbohydrate; 26.3g protein; 0.9g fibre
tips You will need to soak eight bamboo skewers in water for at least an hour to prevent them from splintering and scorching.
The sauce can be used as a marinade for the chicken before cooking, but cook chicken on medium heat so marinade does not burn before meat cooks through. You can also use ready-made yakitori sauce, available from Asian grocery stores.
You can substitute seven-spice mix for japanese pepper.
Chicken wings, chicken liver or vegetables of your choice can be used in this dish, but remember to cut even-sized pieces and use ingredients that take about the same time to cook.

Grilled miso chicken

8 chicken thigh fillets (1.2kg)
2 tablespoons light soy sauce
2 tablespoons sake
2 tablespoons mirin
2 tablespoons white miso
2 green onions (scallions), chopped finely
1cm (½-inch) piece fresh ginger (5g), grated
1 clove garlic, crushed

1 Place chicken and combined remaining ingredients in shallow dish, rubbing marinade all over chicken. Cover; refrigerate 1 hour.
2 Drain chicken; reserve marinade. Cook chicken on heated oiled grill plate (or grill or barbecue), brushing with reserved marinade, about 6 minutes on each side or until cooked through.
3 Serve chicken with steamed rice and a sprinkle of seven-spice mix, if you like.

prep + cook time 15 minutes (+ refrigeration) **serves** 8
nutritional count per serving 11.2g total fat (3.4g saturated fat); 953kJ (228 cal); 1.7g carbohydrate; 28.9g protein; 0.4g fibre

Slow-roasted duck with citrus peaches

1.8kg (3½ pounds) duck
2 teaspoons sea salt flakes
1 teaspoon sesame oil
10 cloves garlic
80g (2½ ounces) fresh ginger, sliced
3 pieces lemon rind
800g (1½ pounds) kipfler (fingerling) potatoes, halved lengthways
2 bay leaves
¼ cup (60ml) rice vinegar
2 tablespoons caster (superfine) sugar
2 tablespoons water
3 medium peaches (450g), cut into quarters

1 Preheat oven to 120°C/250°F.
2 Wash duck under cold water; pat dry inside and out with absorbent paper. Prick skin with skewer (without piercing flesh). Place duck, breast-side up, on wire rack in large roasting dish; rub inside and out with salt and oil. Place garlic, ginger and 2 pieces of the rind inside duck cavity. Roast, uncovered, 2 hours.
3 Remove roasting dish from oven. Increase oven to 200°C/400°F.
4 Place potato and leaves in another large roasting dish. Pour duck fat over potatoes; toss to coat. Return duck to oven with potatoes; roast 45 minutes.
5 Remove duck from oven. Cover loosely with foil; stand 15 minutes. Meanwhile, roast potatoes another 15 minutes.
6 Shred remaining piece of rind. Add rind, vinegar, sugar and the water to frying pan over heat; stir, without boiling, until sugar dissolves. Bring to the boil. Reduce heat; simmer, without stirring, until pale golden. Add peaches; cook until slightly soft.
7 Serve duck pieces with roasted potatoes and peaches.

prep + cook time 3 hours **serves** 4
nutritional count per serving 68.4g total fat (20.2g saturated fat); 4263kJ (1020 cal); 41.8g carbohydrate; 56.7g protein; 6.7g fibre

Crisp duck breast with orange and daikon salad

3 medium oranges (720g)
300g (9½ ounces) daikon
1½ tablespoons vegetable oil
1 teaspoon sesame oil
1 tablespoon sake
4 duck breasts (800g), skin scored
1 teaspoon salt
80g (2½ ounces) rocket (arugula) or mizuna
ponzu dressing
5cm (2-inch) piece kelp (konbu), shredded
1 tablespoon japanese soy sauce
1 tablespoon sake
1 teaspoon rice vinegar
1 teaspoon mirin
1 teaspoon bonito flakes

1 Make ponzu dressing.
2 Segment orange over salad bowl; reserve 1 tablespoon of juice.
Using vegetable peeler, slice daikon into ribbons.
3 Strain ponzu dressing into small bowl; add oils, sake and reserved juice.
4 Season duck with salt, rubbing well into skin. Cook duck, skin-side
down, in heated oiled frying pan until skin is golden. Remove from pan;
discard fat. Return duck to same pan; cook until cooked to your liking.
Remove duck from pan; stand, covered, 5 minutes. Slice thinly.
5 Meanwhile, place drained orange in medium bowl with daikon and
rocket; toss gently to combine.
6 Serve duck with salad; drizzle with dressing.
ponzu dressing Combine ingredients in small non-metallic bowl.
Refrigerate overnight.

prep + cook time 30 minutes (+ refrigeration) **serves** 4
nutritional count per serving 60.4g total fat (16.6g saturated fat);
3214kJ (769 cal); 12.4g carbohydrate; 41.6g protein; 3.9g fibre

Teriyaki chicken rice burger

1½ cups (300g) japanese rice (koshihikari)
2 teaspoons white sesame seeds
cooking-oil spray
2 teaspoons vegetable oil
4 chicken thigh fillets (600g), skin on
¼ cup (60ml) japanese soy sauce
2 tablespoons mirin
2 tablespoons sake
1½ tablespoons caster (superfine) sugar
1 lebanese cucumber (130g), cut into ribbons
20g (¾ ounce) rocket (arugula) or mizuna
2 tablespoons mayonnaise

1 Preheat oven to 200°C/400°F.
2 Cook rice in large saucepan of boiling water until tender; drain. Spread warm rice in lightly oiled 40cm x 25cm (16-inch x 10-inch) baking tray; smooth surface with damp hands. Sprinkle with seeds; press down to adhere. Cool to room temperature.
3 Cut rounds from rice using 9cm (3¾-inch) cutter; place on oven tray lined with baking (parchment) paper. Spray with cooking oil; bake 15 minutes. Turn; bake another 15 minutes or until slightly crisp. Keep warm.
4 Meanwhile, heat oil in large frying pan; cook chicken, skin-side down, until golden. Turn; cook until browned and cooked through. Remove from pan.
5 Bring sauce, mirin, sake and sugar to the boil in same pan. Reduce heat; simmer until sauce thickens. Return chicken to pan; turn to coat.
6 Sandwich chicken, cucumber, rocket and mayonnaise between rice rounds.

prep + cook time 1 hour (+ cooling) **serves** 4
nutritional count per serving 17.2g total fat (4g saturated fat); 1492kJ (357 cal); 17.5g carbohydrate; 30.1g protein; 0.8g fibre
tip Any leftover rice is perfect for making fried rice.

Teriyaki duck with wombok and daikon salad

10 dried shiitake mushrooms
3 litres (12 cups) water
1.5 litres (6 cups) chicken stock
1 cup (250ml) sake
1 cup (250ml) mirin
½ cup (125ml) japanese soy sauce
½ cup (110g) firmly packed
   dark brown sugar
¼ cup (60ml) tamari
6 green onions (scallions), halved
3 cloves garlic, quartered
5cm (2-inch) piece fresh ginger
   (25g), unpeeled, chopped
2kg (4 pounds) duck
2 tablespoons teriyaki sauce
1 tablespoon japanese soy sauce,
   extra

wombok and daikon salad
2 tablespoons white miso
1 tablespoon mirin
1 tablespoon sake
1 tablespoon sugar
¼ cup (60ml) rice vinegar
1 teaspoon japanese soy sauce
2 small carrots (140g),
   cut into matchsticks
½ small daikon (200g), halved
   lengthways, sliced thinly
½ small wombok (napa cabbage)
   (350g), shredded
3 green onions (scallions),
   chopped coarsely
1 fresh long red chilli, sliced thinly

1 Place mushrooms in small heatproof bowl, cover with boiling water, stand 20 minutes; drain. Discard stems; slice caps thickly.
2 Place mushrooms, the water, stock, sake, mirin, sauce, sugar, tamari, onion, garlic and ginger in stock pot with duck; bring to the boil. Reduce heat; simmer, uncovered, 1 hour or until duck is cooked through. Remove from heat; stand duck in cooking liquid 2 hours or until cool. Remove duck from liquid; stand on wire rack 2 hours (discard liquid). Cut duck into quarters.
3 Make wombok and daikon salad.
4 Brush combined teriyaki and 1 tablespoon extra japanese soy over duck skin. Cook duck, skin-side down, on heated oiled grill plate (or grill or barbecue) 5 minutes. Turn duck skin-side up; brush with remaining teriyaki mixture. Cover; cook duck until heated through. Serve duck with salad.
wombok and daikon salad Stir miso, mirin, sake and sugar in small pan over heat, without boiling, until sugar dissolves. Remove from heat; stir in vinegar and sauce. Combine dressing and remaining ingredients in bowl.

prep + cook time 1 hour 55 minutes (+ standing & cooling) **serves** 4
nutritional count per serving 94.8g total fat (28.7g saturated fat); 5488kJ (1313 cal); 48.6g carbohydrate; 44.2g protein; 4.6g fibre

Sake marinated quail

12 quails (2kg)
¾ cup (180ml) sake
⅔ cup (160ml) sweet sherry
½ cup (110g) light brown sugar
⅓ cup (80ml) light soy sauce
2 tablespoons mirin
3 green onions (scallions), chopped
8cm (3-inch) piece fresh ginger (40g), grated
4 cloves garlic, crushed
vegetable oil, for deep-frying
1 tablespoon cornflour (cornstarch)
½ cup (125ml) chicken stock

1 Tie quail legs with string; tuck wings under body. Bring large saucepan of water to the boil, add quail to water in batches, simmer 2 minutes; drain quail, discard water.
2 Combine quails, sake, sherry, sugar, sauce, mirin, onion, ginger and garlic in large bowl. Cover; refrigerate 4 hours or overnight, turning quails occasionally.
3 Drain quails; reserve marinade. Heat oil in large saucepan; deep-fry quails, in batches, until browned and tender. Remove from pan. Drain on absorbent paper; keep warm.
4 Meanwhile, bring reserved marinade to the boil in frying pan. Reduce heat; simmer until reduced by one-third. Stir in blended cornflour and stock; stir until sauce boils and thickens.
5 Serve quail with sauce.

prep + cook time 25 minutes (+ refrigeration) **serves** 6
nutritional count per serving 27.7g total fat (6g saturated fat); 2157kJ (516 cal); 23.4g carbohydrate; 32.3g protein; 0.4g fibre

Sake chicken

800g (1½ pounds) chicken breast fillets
½ cup (125ml) sake
2 tablespoons rice vinegar
2 tablespoons japanese soy sauce
1 tablespoon lemon juice
2 teaspoons sesame oil
1 teaspoon caster (superfine) sugar
1 clove garlic, crushed
1 fresh long red chilli, chopped finely
2 green onions (scallions), sliced thinly
2 tablespoons (46g) drained pink pickled ginger,
  shredded finely

1 Place chicken, sake, vinegar, sauce, juice, oil, sugar, garlic and chilli in large frying pan; bring to the boil. Reduce heat; simmer, covered, about 10 minutes or until chicken is cooked through. Remove from heat; stand chicken in poaching liquid 10 minutes before slicing thickly. Cover to keep warm.
2 Bring poaching liquid to the boil; boil, uncovered, about 5 minutes or until sauce thickens.
3 Serve chicken drizzled with sauce; top with onion and ginger.

prep + cook time 25 minutes **serves** 4
nutritional count per serving 13.4g total fat (3.7g saturated fat); 1413kJ (338 cal); 4.4g carbohydrate; 43.7g protein; 0.5g fibre

Sake duck with snow peas and avocado

100g (3 ounces) snow peas
½ medium red capsicum (bell pepper) (100g), sliced thinly
1 tablespoon olive oil
200g (6½ ounces) single duck breast fillet
¼ cup (60ml) sake
2 tablespoons light soy sauce
1 tablespoon brown sugar
1 tablespoon rice vinegar
½ small avocado (100g), chopped

1 Boil, steam or microwave peas and capsicum until just tender; drain.
Rinse under cold water, pat dry with absorbent paper.
2 Heat oil in medium frying pan; cook duck, skin-side down, until skin
is browned and crisp. Turn duck, cook 5 minutes or until duck is tender.
Remove duck from pan; stand 10 minutes, slice thinly.
3 Meanwhile, combine sake, sauce, sugar and vinegar in clean pan;
simmer, uncovered, 2 minutes or until sauce is thick and syrupy.
4 Remove syrup from heat; add duck, turn to coat. Serve duck with
snow peas, capsicum and avocado.

prep + cook time 25 minutes (+ standing) **serves** 2
nutritional count per serving 43.2g total fat (10.8g saturated fat);
2291kJ (548 cal); 11.1g carbohydrate; 23.8g protein; 2.2g fibre

Sesame wasabi chicken with daikon salad

8 chicken drumsticks (1.2kg)
2 tablespoons wasabi paste
1 tablespoon japanese soy sauce
1 tablespoon sesame oil
daikon salad
2 medium carrots (240g)
1 small daikon (400g)
6 green onions (scallions), sliced thinly
2 tablespoons white sesame seeds, toasted
1 tablespoon mirin
1 tablespoon lime juice
2 teaspoons sesame oil
2 teaspoons japanese soy sauce

1 Combine chicken, wasabi, sauce and oil in large bowl.
2 Cook chicken mixture on oiled heated grill plate (or grill or barbecue), turning and brushing occasionally with marinade, about 40 minutes or until cooked through.
3 Meanwhile, make daikon salad.
4 Serve chicken with salad.
daikon salad Using vegetable peeler, slice carrots and daikon into ribbons. Place in large bowl with remaining ingredients; toss gently to combine.

prep + cook time 1 hour **serves** 4
nutritional count per serving 31.3g total fat (7.7g saturated fat); 1948kJ (466 cal); 7.2g carbohydrate; 36.5g protein; 4.1g fibre

Beef & Lamb

Pepper steak with ginger mashed potatoes

4 small potatoes (480g), cut into chunks
15g (½ ounce) butter
½ cup (125ml) milk, warm
¼ cup (60ml) double cream
1 teaspoon potato flour
3 teaspoons water
2 tablespoons japanese soy sauce
2 tablespoons mirin
2.5cm (1-inch) piece fresh ginger (15g), grated
4 beef fillet steaks (740g)
2 tablespoons japanese pepper

1 Boil, steam or microwave potato until tender; drain. Mash potato with butter and milk in large bowl until smooth. Stir in cream; cover to keep warm.
2 Meanwhile, whisk flour and the water in small bowl until smooth. Bring sauce and mirin to the boil in small saucepan. Stir in flour mixture; simmer until thickened. Remove from heat; stir in ginger.
3 Season steaks with japanese pepper and a little salt. Heat oiled frying pan; cook steaks until done to your liking. Remove from pan; stand 2 minutes, covered, to keep warm.
4 Divide mashed potato among serving plates, top with steak; pour over sauce. Sprinkle with chopped green onion, if you like.

prep + cook time 30 minutes **serves** 4
nutritional count per serving 20.9g total fat (11.5g saturated fat); 1881kJ (450 cal); 17.8g carbohydrate; 43.9g protein; 2.5g fibre
tip Have the steaks at room temperature before you cook them.

Sesame-roasted steak

2 tablespoons white sesame seeds, toasted
2 tablespoons japanese soy sauce
1 tablespoon sake
1 teaspoon caster (superfine) sugar
2.5cm (1-inch) piece fresh ginger (15g), grated
1 clove garlic, crushed
4 beef scotch fillet steaks (800g)
3 green onions (scallions), cut into short thin strips
1 tablespoon olive oil
chilli dressing
¼ cup (60ml) japanese soy sauce
1 teaspoons dashi granules
¼ teaspoon seven-spice mix
2cm (¾-inch) piece fresh ginger (10g), sliced finely

1 Blend, process or grind seeds until coarse. Combine seeds, sauce, sake, sugar, ginger and garlic in shallow dish with steaks. Cover; refrigerate 30 minutes.
2 Meanwhile, make chilli dressing.
3 Place onion in small bowl, cover with iced water, stand 10 minutes or until crisp and curled; drain.
4 Heat oil in large frying pan; cook steaks until done to your liking. Remove from pan; stand 5 minutes, covered, to keep warm. Slice thickly.
5 Arrange sliced steaks on serving plate; drizzle over dressing. Top with onion. Serve on steamed rice, if you like.
chilli dressing Combine ingredients in small bowl.

prep + cook time 45 minutes (+ refrigeration) **serves** 4
nutritional count per serving 17.3g total fat (5.2g saturated fat); 1459kJ (349 cal); 2g carbohydrate; 44.6g protein; 0.7g fibre

Beef, shiitake and red wine stew

300g (9½ ounces) fresh shiitake mushrooms
¼ cup (60ml) vegetable oil
9 tiny leeks (400g), cut into chunks
1 large brown onion (200g), chopped
1 large carrot (180g), chopped
4 rindless bacon slices (260g), chopped
2 tablespoons plain (all-purpose) flour
1 teaspoon japanese pepper
sea salt flakes
1kg (2 pounds) beef chuck steak, cut into chunks
3 cloves garlic, crushed
1½ cups (375ml) red wine
1½ cups (375ml) sake
2 tablespoons red miso
1 cup (250ml) water

1 Discard mushroom stems; halve caps.
2 Heat 1 tablespoon of the oil in large saucepan; cook leeks, stirring, until softened. Remove from pan.
3 Heat 2 teaspoons of the oil in same pan; cook mushrooms, stirring, until softened and lightly browned. Remove from pan; add to leeks.
4 Add onion, carrot and bacon to same pan; cook stirring, until lightly browned. Remove from pan.
5 Combine flour, pepper and a pinch of sea salt in large bowl. Coat steak in seasoned flour; shake off excess. Heat remaining oil in same pan; cook steak, in batches, until browned. Remove from pan.
6 Add garlic to same pan; cook until fragrant. Add red wine and sake, scraping up any brown bits from base of pan. Return beef and any juices to pan with onion, carrot, bacon, miso and the water, stirring until miso dissolves; bring to the boil. Reduce heat; simmer, covered, 1½ hours. Add leek and mushrooms; simmer, covered, about 30 minutes or until beef is tender and sauce has thickened slightly.

prep + cook time 3 hours **serves** 6
nutritional count per serving 26.4g total fat (7.5g saturated fat); 2395kJ (573 cal); 10.5g carbohydrate; 50.8g protein; 4.7g fibre
tip Serve this stew with mashed potato or steamed rice.

Veal cutlets with vegetable hot pot and soy mayonnaise

¼ cup (60ml) vegetable oil
1 teaspoon sesame oil
1 medium leek (350g), chopped
2cm (¾-inch) piece fresh
   ginger (10g), grated
2 cloves garlic, crushed
3 baby eggplants (180g), chopped
2 medium zucchini (240g),
   chopped
1 medium red capsicum (bell
   pepper) (200g), chopped
100g (3 ounces) fresh shiitake
   mushrooms, chopped

¼ cup (60ml) mirin
¾ cup (185ml) tomato puree
¼ cup (60ml) rice vinegar
pinch of caster (superfine) sugar
¼ cup (60ml) water
½ sheet seaweed (nori), shredded
4 veal cutlets (500g)
soy mayonnaise
2 teaspoons white miso
½ teaspoon japanese soy sauce
1 clove garlic, crushed
½ cup (125g) mayonnaise

1 Combine oils in small bowl. Heat 2 tablespoons of oil mixture in large deep frying pan; cook leek, stirring, until softened. Add ginger and garlic; cook, stirring, until fragrant. Add remaining vegetables; cook, stirring, until softened. Stir in mirin; cook 1 minute. Stir in tomato puree, vinegar, sugar and the water; bring to the boil. Reduce heat; simmer, covered, 20 minutes until vegetables are tender. Stir through seaweed.
2 Heat remaining oil mixture in large frying pan; cook cutlets until done to your liking.
3 Meanwhile, make soy mayonnaise.
4 Serve cutlets with vegetable hot pot and mayonnaise.
soy mayonnaise Whisk miso, sauce and garlic in small bowl until smooth; whisk in mayonnaise.

prep + cook time 45 minutes **serves** 4
nutritional count per serving 29.3g total fat (4.6g saturated fat); 2048kJ (490 cal); 15.9g carbohydrate; 35.7g protein; 6.3g fibre

Ginger teriyaki beef

⅓ cup (80ml) teriyaki sauce
½ cup (125ml) hoisin sauce
2 tablespoons mirin
1 tablespoon peanut oil
750g (1½ pounds) beef strips
250g (8 ounces) broccoli, cut into florets
250g (11 ounces) sugar snap peas, trimmed
115g (3½ ounces) fresh baby corn, halved lengthways
4cm (1½-inch) piece fresh ginger (20g), grated
1½ cups (120g) bean sprouts, trimmed

1 Combine sauces and mirin in small jug.
2 Heat half of the oil in wok; stir-fry beef, in batches, until browned.
3 Heat remaining oil in wok; stir-fry broccoli until tender.
4 Return beef to wok with sauce mixture, peas, corn and ginger; stir-fry until vegetables and beef are cooked. Remove from heat; sprinkle with sprouts.

prep + cook time 25 minutes **serves** 4
nutritional count per serving 17.6g total fat (5.1g saturated fat); 1948kJ (466 cal); 23.8g carbohydrate; 47.6g protein; 9g fibre

Beef teriyaki platter

600g (1 ¼ pounds) sirloin steaks, trimmed
⅓ cup (80ml) teriyaki sauce
2.5cm (1-inch) piece fresh ginger (15g), grated
1 clove garlic, crushed
500g (1 pound) thick asparagus, trimmed
8 thick green onions (scallions), trimmed
1 teaspoon wasabi paste
¼ cup (60ml) japanese soy sauce

1 Combine steaks, teriyaki sauce, ginger and garlic in large bowl. Cover; refrigerate 3 hours or overnight.
2 Drain steaks; discard marinade. Cook steaks on heated oiled grill plate (or grill or barbecue) until cooked as desired. Transfer steaks to warm plate; cover, stand 5 minutes.
3 Meanwhile, cook asparagus and onions on heated oiled grill plate (or grill or barbecue) until tender.
4 Slice steaks thinly; place on warmed serving platter with asparagus, green onions, wasabi and sauce. Serve with steamed rice, if you like.

prep + cook time 30 minutes (+ refrigeration) **serves** 4
nutritional count per serving 11.6g total fat (4.4g saturated fat); 1099kJ (263 cal); 4.7g carbohydrate; 34g protein; 1.7g fibre

Beef and vegetable rolls

2 medium carrots (240g)
6 asparagus spears, halved lengthways
3 green onions (scallions)
12 thin slices beef eye fillet (300g)
2 tablespoons cornflour (cornstarch)
1 tablespoon vegetable oil
1 tablespoon sugar
¼ cup (60ml) mirin
2 tablespoons sake
¼ cup (60ml) japanese soy sauce

1 Using a vegetable peeler, slice carrot lengthways into thin strips.
Cut carrot strips to width of beef.
2 Boil, steam or microwave asparagus until just tender; drain. Rinse
under cold water, drain. Cut asparagus and onions to width of beef.
3 Place beef slices flat on work surface; sift half the cornflour over top of
beef. Place two pieces of carrot and onion, and one piece of asparagus
across dusted side of each slice of beef; roll up. Tie rolls with kitchen
string or secure ends with toothpicks. Dust with remaining cornflour.
4 Heat oil in medium frying pan; cook rolls, in batches, until browned
all over. Remove from pan.
5 Return rolls to same cleaned pan, add combined sugar, mirin, sake
and sauce; bring to the boil. Reduce heat; simmer, turning occasionally,
until rolls are cooked through. (If you prefer a thicker sauce, remove rolls;
boil sauce until reduced. Return rolls to pan; turn to coat in sauce.)
6 Remove rolls from pan; cool 2 minutes. Discard string or toothpicks;
cut rolls in half. Serve with sauce.

prep + cook time 30 minutes **serves** 4
nutritional count per serving 8.3g total fat (2.2g saturated fat);
907kJ (217 cal); 12.9g carbohydrate; 17.8g protein; 2g fibre
tips Very thinly sliced beef, sold as yakiniku or sukiyaki beef, is available
from Asian grocery stores.
You could use rib eye steak (scotch fillet) instead of the beef eye fillet.
Pork fillet can be used instead of beef eye fillet, if you like.
To make larger rolls, use two or three slices of meat, slightly overlapping.

Seared beef

½ small daikon (200g), shredded finely
400g (12½ ounces) beef eye fillet
1 lebanese cucumber (130g)
ponzu sauce
¼ cup (60ml) lemon juice
¼ cup (60ml) japanese soy sauce
¼ cup (60ml) primary dashi (see recipe page 116)
2 green onions (scallions), sliced thinly

1 Place daikon in medium bowl, cover with cold water, stand 15 minutes; drain.
2 Meanwhile, make ponzu sauce.
3 Cook beef on heated oiled grill plate (or grill or barbecue) until browned all over. Allow to cool (or plunge into cold water to stop cooking immediately). Drain; pat dry with absorbent paper.
4 Halve cucumber lengthways; discard seeds with teaspoon. Slice cucumber thinly. Cut beef into thin slices; arrange on serving plate with mounds of daikon and cucumber. Serve with ponzu sauce.
ponzu sauce Combine juice, sauce and dashi in small bowl; sprinkle with onion.

prep + cook time 20 minutes (+ standing) **serves** 4
nutritional count per serving 5g total fat (2.1g saturated fat); 635kJ (152 cal); 2.7g carbohydrate; 22.5g protein; 1.1g fibre
tips You could use rib eye steak (scotch fillet) or rump steak instead of the beef eye fillet. The beef in this recipe is raw in the middle.
Serve with separate bowls of finely chopped garlic, grated fresh ginger, lemon wedges and japanese soy sauce.

Mixed barbecue (teppanyaki)

4 uncooked large king prawns
  (shrimp) (280g)
500g (1 pound) beef eye fillet,
  sliced thinly
350g (11 ounces) chicken breast
  fillet, skin on, cut into chunks
¼ cup (60ml) japanese soy sauce
2 cloves garlic, crushed
1 fresh red thai chilli (serrano
  chili), seeded, chopped finely
4 fresh shiitake mushrooms
1 medium onion (150g), sliced thinly
1 medium red capsicum
  (bell pepper) (200g),
  seeded and chopped
4 green onions (scallions),
  chopped finely

dipping sauce
½ cup (125ml) japanese
  soy sauce
1 tablespoon mirin
1 tablespoon light brown sugar
2cm (¾-inch) piece fresh ginger
  (20g), grated
½ teaspoon sesame oil

1 Shell and devein prawns, leaving tails intact. Combine prawns with
beef, chicken, sauce, garlic and chilli in large bowl; stand 15 minutes.
2 Meanwhile, make dipping sauce.
3 Discard mushroom stems; cut a cross in the top of caps.
4 Cook ingredients, except green onions, in batches, on heated oiled
grill plate (or grill or barbecue) until vegetables are just tender, prawns
and beef are cooked as you like and chicken is cooked through.
5 Serve with green onion and individual bowls of dipping sauce.
dipping sauce Stir ingredients in medium saucepan until sugar dissolves.

prep + cook time 40 minutes **serves** 4
nutritional count per serving 11.8g total fat (4.2g saturated fat);
1580kJ (378 cal); 8.8g carbohydrate; 56.5g protein; 1.7g fibre
tips You could use rump or sirloin steak instead of the beef eye fillet.
Teppanyaki is traditionally cooked on a grill plate on or near the table,
and is eaten in batches; a portable electric grill is ideal for this.

Teriyaki lamb with carrot salad

600g (1 ¼ pounds) diced lamb
2 tablespoons japanese soy sauce
2 tablespoons mirin
1 teaspoon caster (superfine) sugar
9 green onions (scallions)
carrot salad
2 medium carrots (240g), cut into matchsticks
1 cup (80g) bean sprouts, trimmed
1 small red onion (100g), sliced thinly
1 tablespoon white sesame seeds, toasted
2 teaspoons japanese soy sauce
1 tablespoon mirin
½ teaspoon sugar
2 teaspoons peanut oil

1 Combine lamb, sauce, mirin and sugar in medium bowl.
2 Cut four 3cm (1 ¼-inch) long pieces from trimmed root end of each onion.
3 Thread lamb and onion pieces, alternately, onto 12 bamboo skewers. Cook skewers on heated oiled grill plate (or grill or barbecue), brushing with soy mixture occasionally, until lamb is cooked as you like.
4 Meanwhile, make carrot salad.
5 Serve skewers with salad.
carrot salad Place ingredients in medium bowl; toss gently to combine.

prep + cook time 35 minutes **serves** 4
nutritional count per serving 12.5g total fat (4.7g saturated fat); 1200kJ (287 cal); 7.1g carbohydrate; 32.9g protein; 2.9g fibre
tip You will need to soak 12 bamboo skewers in water for at least an hour to prevent them from splintering and scorching.

Sukiyaki

200g (6½ ounces) firm tofu
400g (12½ ounces) fresh gelatinous noodles, drained
8 fresh shiitake mushrooms
600g (1¼ pounds) beef rump steak
4 green onions (scallions), chopped finely
300g (9½ ounces) spinach, trimmed, chopped coarsely
125g (4 ounces) can bamboo shoots, drained, sliced thinly
4 eggs
broth
1 cup (250ml) japanese soy sauce
½ cup (125ml) sake
½ cup (125ml) mirin
½ cup (125ml) water
½ cup (110g) caster (superfine) sugar

1 Press tofu between two chopping boards with weight on top, raise one end; stand 25 minutes. Cut tofu into 2cm (¾-inch) cubes.
2 Meanwhile, make broth.
3 Rinse noodles under hot water; drain. Cut into 15cm (6-inch) lengths.
4 Discard mushroom stems; cut a cross in top of caps.
5 Trim beef of all fat; slice thinly. Retain a small piece of beef fat for greasing sukiyaki pan. Arrange ingredients on platters or in bowls. Place broth in medium bowl. Break eggs into individual bowls; beat lightly.
6 Heat greased sukiyaki pan (or electric frying pan) on a portable gas cooker at the table; add one-quarter of the beef, stir-fry until partly cooked. Add a quarter each of the vegetables, tofu, noodles and broth. Dip cooked ingredients in egg before eating.
7 As ingredients and broth are eaten, add remaining ingredients and broth to pan, in batches.
broth Stir ingredients in saucepan over medium heat until sugar dissolves.

prep + cook time 30 minutes **serves** 4
nutritional count per serving 17.2g total fat (5.5g saturated fat); 2521kJ (603 cal); 44.6g carbohydrate; 54.9g protein; 6.5g fibre
tips You could use beef sirloin or rib eye (scotch fillet) instead of the rump steak. Sukiyaki beef is available fresh and frozen from Asian grocery stores and selected supermarkets.
A traditional sukiyaki pan is available from Japanese stores.

Shabu-shabu

300g (9½ ounces) firm tofu
400g (12½ ounces) fresh
gelatinous noodles, drained
12 fresh shiitake mushrooms
(180g)
600g (1¼ pounds) beef eye fillet,
sliced thinly
4 tiny leeks (320g), halved
lengthways, sliced diagonally
into 2cm (¾-inch) pieces
6 wombok (napa cabbage) leaves,
chopped coarsely
100g (3 ounces) bamboo shoots,
sliced thinly

12 small pieces decorative
wheat gluten (fu)
4 green onions (scallions),
chopped finely
1 quantity ponzu sauce
(see recipe page 273)
10cm (4-inch) piece kelp (konbu),
cut into quarters
1.5 litres (6 cups) water
red maple radish
120g (4 ounces) daikon, peeled
4 hot dried red chillies, seeded

1 Press tofu between two chopping boards with weight on top, raise
one end; stand 25 minutes. Cut tofu into 2cm (¾-inch) cubes.
2 Rinse noodles under hot water, drain; cut into 20cm (8-inch) lengths.
3 Discard mushroom stems; cut a cross in the top of caps.
4 Arrange beef, tofu, vegetables and decorative wheat gluten on a platter.
5 Make red maple radish.
6 Divide ponzu sauce amoung individual serving dishes; place mound
of red maple radish on sauce.
7 Make a few cuts along edges of kelp; place in 2-litre (8-cup) flameproof
dish or pot with 1.125 litres (4½ cups) of the water. Bring to the boil.
Remove kelp just before water boils. Reduce heat; simmer 4 minutes.
8 Add a selection of ingredients from platter to the broth. As soon as
they are cooked, remove and dip in red maple radish and ponzu sauce.
Add more ingredients and remaining water as required. Skim surface of
broth periodically to remove scum.
red maple radish Using a chopstick, poke four holes in one end of
daikon; insert a chilli into each hole. Grate daikon and chillies in a circular
motion with a Japanese or fine-toothed grater. Squeeze out excess liquid.

prep + cook time 30 minutes **serves** 4
nutritional count per serving 13.7g total fat (3.9g saturated fat);
1835kJ (439 cal); 26.7g carbohydrate; 46.4g protein; 10.8g fibre

Pork

Slow-cooked pork

2 teaspoons vegetable oil
1kg (2 pounds) boneless pork belly, cut into chunks
10cm (4-inch) piece fresh ginger (100g), sliced thickly
2 cups (500ml) secondary dashi (see recipe page 117)
⅔ cup (160ml) sake
½ cup (125ml) japanese soy sauce
⅓ cup (75g) firmly packed dark brown sugar
¼ cup (60ml) mirin

1 Heat oil in large saucepan; cook pork, in batches, 5 minutes or until browned. Rinse pork under hot water to remove excess oil; discard fat from saucepan.
2 Return pork to same pan with ginger and enough cold water to cover; bring to the boil. Reduce heat; simmer, uncovered, 2 hours, topping up with more water if necessary. Strain pork; discard liquid and ginger.
3 Stir dashi, sake, sauce, sugar and mirin in medium saucepan over heat, without boiling, until sugar dissolves. Add pork; bring to the boil. Reduce heat; simmer, uncovered, 1 hour, turning occasionally until pork is tender. Remove from heat; stand 20 minutes. Remove pork from pan; cover to keep warm.
4 Bring cooking liquid to the boil. Reduce heat; simmer, uncovered, 5 minutes or until sauce thickens slightly. Return pork to pan; turn to coat in sauce.

prep + cook time 3 hours 30 minutes (+ standing) **serves** 4
nutritional count per serving 25.1g total fat (9g saturated fat); 2144kJ (513 cal); 20.3g carbohydrate; 43.5g protein; 0g fibre
tip Serve pork with steamed rice and asian greens, and japanese mustard on the side, if you like.

Pork curry

25g (¾ ounce) butter
1 teaspoon sesame oil
1 tablespoon vegetable oil
1 large brown onion (200g), sliced thickly
750g (1½ pounds) pork shoulder, cut into chunks
2 cloves garlic, crushed
1½ tablespoons japanese curry powder
1½ cups (375ml) secondary dashi (see recipe page 117)
¼ cup (60ml) white miso
2 tablespoons mirin
1 tablespoon japanese soy sauce
2½ cups (625ml) water
2 large potatoes (600g), chopped coarsely
2 medium carrots (240g), chopped coarsely
100g (3 ounces) green beans, chopped coarsely

1 Heat butter, sesame oil and half the vegetable oil in large saucepan; cook onion, stirring, until softened. Remove from pan.
2 Heat remaining vegetable oil in same pan; cook pork, in batches, until browned. Remove from pan; set aside with onions.
3 Add garlic and curry powder to same pan; cook, stirring, until fragrant. Return onion and pork to pan; stir to coat in powder.
4 Stir in dashi, miso, mirin, sauce and the water; bring to the boil. Reduce heat; simmer, covered, 1 hour. Add potato and carrot; simmer, uncovered, 45 minutes until potatoes are tender. Add beans; cook, 5 minutes until beans are tender.

prep + cook time 2 hours 15 minutes **serves** 4
nutritional count per serving 19.6g total fat (7g saturated fat); 2073kJ (496 cal); 28g carbohydrate; 48.2g protein; 6.1g fibre
tips Serve curry with steamed rice or noodles, if you like.
If japanese curry powder is unavailable, any mild flavoured curry powder can be used.

Pan-fried pork cutlets with nashi

2 medium nashi pears (400g)
20g (¾ ounce) butter
1 teaspoon vegetable oil
1 teaspoon sesame oil
4 pork cutlets (940g)
⅓ cup (80ml) chicken stock
¼ cup (60ml) mirin
1 tablespoon rice vinegar
1 clove garlic, crushed
½ teaspoon japanese mustard
⅔ cup (160ml) pouring cream
2 japanese mint (shiso) leaves, sliced finely

1 Trim top and base of nashi; discard ends. Slice each nashi, crossways, into quarters. Heat butter in large frying pan; cook nashi, in batches, about 2 minutes or until just tender and browned. Remove from pan; cover to keep warm.
2 Heat combined oils in same pan; cook cutlets, in batches, until browned both sides. Remove from pan; cover to keep warm.
3 Add stock, mirin, vinegar and garlic to same pan; bring to the boil. Reduce heat; stir in mustard, cream and any juices from resting cutlets. Simmer about 2 minutes until sauce thickens slightly.
4 Serve cutlets with nashi slices and sauce; sprinkle with mint.

prep + cook time 25 minutes **serves** 4
nutritional count per serving 30.1g total fat (16.9g saturated fat); 1906kJ (456 cal); 11.8g carbohydrate; 32g protein; 2g fibre
tips If shiso leaves are unavailable, substitute them with basil leaves. Cutlets can also be served with steamed greens or a green salad, if you like.

Tonkatsu

300g (9½ ounces) cabbage, shredded finely
4 pork steaks (600g)
¼ cup (35g) plain (all-purpose) flour
2 eggs, beaten lightly
2 teaspoons water
2 cups (100g) japanese breadcrumbs
vegetable oil, for deep-frying
1 medium lemon (140g), cut into wedges
3 teaspoons japanese mustard
tonkatsu sauce
⅓ cup (80ml) tomato sauce
2 tablespoons japanese worcestershire sauce
2 tablespoons sake
1 teaspoon japanese soy sauce
1 teaspoon japanese mustard

1 Place cabbage in large bowl, cover with iced water, stand 5 minutes until crisp; drain.
2 Meanwhile, make tonkatsu sauce.
3 Pound pork gently with meat mallet. Coat steak in flour; shake off excess. Dip pork in combined egg and the water; coat in breadcrumbs.
4 Heat enough oil to cover pork in medium saucepan or deep-fryer. Cook pork, in batches, turning occasionally, 5 minutes until golden all over (skim oil between batches to remove any crumbs); drain on absorbent paper. Cut pork diagonally into 2cm (¾-inch) slices.
5 Place cabbage on serving plate; arrange pork slices on cabbage. Serve with lemon wedges, mustard and tonkatsu sauce.
tonkatsu sauce Bring ingredients to the boil in small saucepan; whisk until smooth. Remove from heat; cool.

prep + cook time 30 minutes **serves** 4
nutritional count per serving 28.8g total fat (5.5g saturated fat); 2412kJ (577 cal); 32.4g carbohydrate; 43g protein; 5.1g fibre
tips Ready-made tonkatsu sauce is also available from Asian food stores. Japanese breadcrumbs are available in two crumb sizes, either size is suitable for this recipe.

Stir-fried pork and ginger cabbage

400g (12½ ounces) pork fillet, cut into strips
¼ cup (60ml) japanese soy sauce
2 tablespoons sake
1 teaspoon sugar
1cm (½-inch) piece fresh ginger (5g), grated
8 large wombok (napa cabbage) leaves
2 tablespoons vegetable oil
3 teaspoons fresh ginger juice

1 Combine pork, sauce, sake, sugar and grated ginger in medium bowl.
Drain pork over small bowl; reserve marinade.
2 Discard thick ribs from wombok, cut leaves into 4cm (1½-inch) squares.
3 Heat oil in wok; stir-fry pork, in batches, until browned. Remove from wok.
4 Return pork to wok with cabbage, reserved marinade and juice;
stir-fry until hot. Serve with steamed rice and top with chopped green
onions, if you like.

prep + cook time 25 minutes **serves** 4
nutritional count per serving 11.6g total fat (2g saturated fat);
915kJ (219 cal); 2.8g carbohydrate; 23.5g protein; 1.7g fibre
tip To obtain ginger juice, squeeze grated fresh ginger into a sieve set
over a bowl. A piece of ginger measuring about 15cm (6 inches) in
length will yield 3 tablespoons of grated ginger; this amount of grated
ginger should in turn yield the 3 teaspoons of juice used in this recipe.

Teriyaki pork with pineapple

600g (1¼ pounds) pork fillets
⅓ cup (80ml) mirin
¼ cup (60ml) japanese soy sauce
2 tablespoons sake
2 teaspoons sugar
5cm (2-inch) piece fresh ginger (25g), grated
2 cloves garlic, crushed
1 small pineapple (900g), sliced thinly
2 green onions (scallions), sliced thinly

1 Combine pork, mirin, sauce, sake, sugar, ginger, garlic in large bowl. Cover; refrigerate 3 hours or overnight.
2 Drain pork over small bowl; reserve marinade. Cook pork on heated oiled grill plate (or grill or barbecue) until browned and cooked to your liking. Remove from grill plate; cover to keep warm.
3 Cook pineapple slices on same grill plate until soft.
4 Bring reserved marinade to the boil in small saucepan; boil 5 minutes or until sauce reduces by half.
5 Serve sliced pork on pineapple, top with onion; drizzle with sauce.

prep + cook time 40 minutes (+ refrigeration) **serves** 4
nutritional count per serving 4.6g total fat (1.4g saturated fat); 1078kJ (258 cal); 12.7g carbohydrate; 35.1g protein; 2.7g fibre

Teriyaki pork with wasabi dressing

750g (1 ½ pounds) pork fillets
¼ cup (60ml) teriyaki marinade
50g (1 ½ ounces) snow pea sprouts
100g (3 ounces) mesclun
1 medium red capsicum (bell pepper) (200g), sliced thinly
250g (8 ounces) yellow teardrop tomatoes, halved
wasabi dressing
1 ½ teaspoons wasabi powder
¼ cup (60ml) cider vinegar
⅓ cup (80ml) vegetable oil
1 tablespoon light soy sauce

1 Brush pork with teriyaki marinade. Cook pork on heated oiled grill plate
(or grill or barbecue), brushing frequently with marinade, until browned
both sides and cooked. Remove from grill plate; cover to keep warm.
2 Meanwhile, make wasabi dressing.
3 Place sprouts, mesclun, capsicum and tomato in large bowl with
dressing; toss gently to combine.
4 Slice pork; serve with salad.
wasabi dressing Whisk powder and vinegar in small jug until combined;
whisk in remaining ingredients.

prep + cook time 25 minutes **serves** 4
nutritional count per serving 24.5g total fat (4g saturated fat);
1822kJ (436 cal); 8.4g carbohydrate; 43.9g protein; 2.5g fibre
tip Ready-made teriyaki marinade is available from Asian food stores
and most supermarkets.

japanese pork stir-fry

2 tablespoons peanut oil
600g (1¼ pounds) pork fillets, sliced thinly
1 large brown onion (200g), sliced thinly
200g (6½ ounces) green beans, chopped coarsely
1 medium red capsicum (bell pepper) (200g), sliced thinly
1 medium green capsicum (bell pepper) (200g), sliced thinly
2 cups (140g) coarsely shredded wombok (nappa cabbage)
¼ cup (60ml) tonkatsu sauce
¼ cup (60ml) sukiyaki sauce

1 Heat half the oil in wok; stir-fry pork, in batches, until browned all over. Remove from wok.
2 Heat remaining oil in wok; stir-fry onion until just tender. Add beans and capsicums; stir-fry until just tender.
3 Return pork to wok with wombok and sauces; stir-fry until wombok just wilts.

prep + cook times 25 minutes **serves** 4
nutritional count per serving 15.9g total fat (3.2g saturated fat); 1409kJ (337 cal); 9.8g carbohydrate; 36.8g protein; 3.6g fibre

Rice & Noodles

Soba noodles with pork, eggplant and chilli

6 green onions (scallions)
¼ cup (60ml) vegetable oil
1 teaspoon sesame oil
3 baby eggplants (180g), sliced thickly
3 cloves garlic, crushed
2cm (¾-inch) piece fresh ginger (10g), grated finely
600g (1¼ pounds) minced (ground) pork
2 tablespoons mirin
2 tablespoons chilli bean paste
1 tablespoon tomato paste
1 tablespoons japanese soy sauce
1 teaspoon light brown sugar
½ teaspoon dashi granules
1 cup (250ml) water
250g (8 ounces) dried soba noodles

1 Slice onion diagonally, keeping white and green part separate.
2 Combine oils in small bowl. Heat 2 tablespoons of the combined oils in wok; stir-fry eggplant until golden. Drain on absorbent paper.
3 Heat remaining combined oils in wok; stir-fry garlic, ginger and white part of the onion until fragrant. Remove from wok.
4 Stir-fry pork in wok until browned, breaking up mince with a fork. Return garlic mixture to wok with mirin, pastes, sauce, sugar, dashi granules and the water; bring to the boil. Reduce heat; simmer 5 minutes.
5 Return eggplant with green part of onion, reserving some for garnish. Simmer 3 minutes until eggplant is tender. Increase heat; boil about 5 minutes until most of liquid has evaporated.
6 Meanwhile, cook noodles in large saucepan of boiling water until tender; drain. Rinse under cold water; drain.
7 Serve noodles topped with meat sauce; sprinkle with reserved onion.

prep + cook time 45 minutes **serves** 4
nutritional count per serving 26.6g total fat (6g saturated fat);
2504kJ (599 cal); 47.9g carbohydrate; 38.3g protein; 4.3g fibre

Chicken and egg on rice

4 dried shiitake mushrooms
½ cup (125ml) secondary dashi (see recipe page 117)
¼ cup (60ml) japanese soy sauce
2 tablespoons mirin
1 teaspoon sugar
100g (3 ounces) chicken breast fillet, sliced thinly
1 small leek (200g), sliced thinly
6 eggs, beaten lightly
4 cups (600g) hot cooked japanese rice (koshihikari)
2 tablespoons finely chopped fresh chives

1 Place mushrooms in small heatproof bowl, cover with boiling water, stand about 20 minutes; drain. Discard stems; halve caps.
2 Meanwhile, bring dashi, sauce, mirin and sugar to the boil in large frying pan. Add chicken, leek and mushrooms; cook, covered, about 3 minutes or until chicken is tender. Pour egg over chicken mixture; cook, covered, over low heat about 2 minutes or until egg just sets.
3 Divide rice among bowls; top with chicken mixture, sprinkle with chives.

prep + cook time 20 minutes (+ standing) **serves** 4
nutritional count per serving 11g total fat (3.2g saturated fat); 1601kJ (383 cal); 46.2g carbohydrate; 22.2g protein; 1.8g fibre
tips You need to cook 1½ cups (300g) of japanese rice for this recipe. The egg mixture should be just set, still a little runny in areas. Remove from heat; keep covered to cook egg a little longer, if you like.

Individual udon casseroles

400g (12½ ounces) dried thick
  udon noodles
200g (6½-ounce) chicken breast
  fillet, chopped coarsely
2 teaspoons japanese soy sauce
2 teaspoons sake
250g (8 ounces) spinach, trimmed
2½ cups (625ml) secondary dashi
  (see recipe page 117)
2 tablespoons light soy sauce

1 tablespoon mirin
1 medium carrot (120g),
  sliced thinly
4 fresh shiitake mushrooms,
  sliced thinly
2 green onions (scallions),
  chopped coarsely
4 eggs
¼ teaspoon seven-spice mix

1 Cook noodles in large saucepan of boiling water until tender; drain. Rinse under cold water, drain.
2 Combine chicken, japanese soy sauce and sake in small bowl; stand 10 minutes.
3 Boil, steam or microwave spinach until just wilted, rinse under cold water; squeeze out excess water, slice thickly.
4 Bring dashi, light soy sauce and mirin to the boil in medium saucepan; keep warm.
5 Place ½ cup (125ml) of the broth in small saucepan, add carrot; cook 2 minutes. Add chicken; cook 2 minutes. Add mushrooms; cook about 1 minute or until chicken is tender.
6 Divide noodles among four 2½-cup (625ml) flameproof dishes; top with carrot, chicken, mushrooms, spinach and onion. Ladel over broth. Cover; bring to the boil. Using the back of a spoon, make a small hollow in noodles; break eggs, one at a time, into small bowl, slide an egg into each hollow. Cover dishes, remove from heat; stand, covered, until egg just sets. Just before serving, sprinkle with seven-spice mix.

prep + cook time 35 minutes (+ standing) **serves** 4
nutritional count per serving 10.3g total fat (3g saturated fat); 2228kJ (533 cal); 71.7g carbohydrate; 33.4g protein; 5.3g fibre
tips Dried udon are available in different thicknesses so cooking times will vary. You could use fresh udon noodles instead; there is no need to cook them before use, rinse under hot water before adding to pan. They are available from most supermarkets.
Japanese use earthenware flameproof pots called donabes. If they are not available, cook in a flameproof dish and serve food at the table.

Sweet soy beef on rice

200g (6½ ounces) gelatinous noodles, drained
½ cup (125ml) japanese soy sauce
1 tablespoon sugar
¼ cup (60ml) mirin
300g (9½-ounce) beef eye fillet, sliced paper thin
2 green onions (scallions), cut into chunks
2 teaspoons fresh ginger juice
5 cups (920g) hot cooked japanese rice (koshihikari)

1 Cook noodles in medium saucepan of boiling water until tender; drain. Cut into 10cm (4 inches) lengths.
2 Bring sauce, sugar and mirin to the boil in medium saucepan. Add beef; cook, stirring, until beef just changes colour. Strain beef over medium heatproof bowl; return sauce to same saucepan.
3 Add onion and noodles to pan; simmer about 3 minutes or until onion softens. Return beef to pan with juice; heat through.
4 Divide rice among serving bowls; top with beef, noodles and ¼ cup of the sauce.

prep + cook time 20 minutes **serves** 4
nutritional count per serving 4.5g total fat (1.6g saturated fat); 2002kJ (479 cal); 81.1g carbohydrate; 24g protein; 1.4g fibre
tips Freeze beef for about an hour – this will make it easier to slice. You need to cook 2 cups (400g) japanese rice for this recipe.
To obtain ginger juice, squeeze grated fresh ginger into a sieve set over a bowl. A piece of ginger measuring about 10cm (4 inches) in length will yield 2 tablespoons of grated ginger; this amount of grated ginger should in turn yield the 2 teaspoons of juice used in this recipe.

Chilled soba with dipping sauce

2 green onions (scallions), chopped finely
1 teaspoon wasabi paste
250g (8 ounces) dried soba noodles
½ sheet toasted seaweed (yaki-nori), sliced thinly
dipping sauce
¾ cup (180ml) primary dashi (see recipe page 116)
2 tablespoons japanese soy sauce
2 tablespoons mirin
½ teaspoon sugar

1 Make dipping sauce. Divide dipping sauce, onion and wasabi among individual side dishes.
2 Cook noodles in large saucepan of boiling water until tender; drain. Rinse under cold water; drain.
3 Just before serving, place noodles in strainer; immerse in iced water to chill. Drain; divide among serving dishes; top with seaweed.
4 Add onion and wasabi to dipping sauce according to taste; dip noodles in sauce before eating.
dipping sauce Stir ingredients in small saucepan over heat until sugar dissolves; cool.

prep + cook time 20 minutes **serves** 4
nutritional count per serving 0.9g total fat (0.2g saturated fat); 966kJ (231 cal); 44.2g carbohydrate; 8.2g protein; 2.2g fibre

Fried soba

250g (8 ounces) dried soba noodles
1 tablespoon sesame oil
2 tablespoons vegetable oil
300g (9½ ounces) minced (ground) pork
1 medium brown onion (150g), cut into eight wedges
1 clove garlic, crushed
1cm (½-inch) piece fresh ginger (5g), grated
500g (1 pound) cabbage, shredded finely
1 medium red capsicum (bell pepper) (200g), sliced thinly
2 tablespoons (46g) drained red pickled ginger
2 teaspoons shredded seaweed (ao-nori)
sauce
¼ cup (60ml) mirin
¼ cup (60ml) japanese soy sauce
2 tablespoons sake
1 tablespoon sugar

1 Cook noodles in large saucepan of boiling water until tender; drain.
2 Make sauce.
3 Heat sesame oil and half the vegetable oil in wok; stir-fry pork until browned lightly. Remove from wok; cover to keep warm.
4 Heat remaining vegetable oil in wok; stir-fry onion, garlic and fresh ginger until onion softens. Add cabbage and capsicum; stir-fry until tender. Add pickled ginger, pork, noodles and sauce; stir-fry until hot. Serve sprinkled with seaweed.
sauce Stir ingredients in small saucepan over heat until sugar dissolves.

prep + cook time 35 minutes **serves** 4
nutritional count per serving 20g total fat (3.9g saturated fat);
2274kJ (544 cal); 57g carbohydrate; 26.1g protein; 7.9g fibre

Soba in broth

200g (6½ ounces) dried soba noodles
3 cups (750ml) primary dashi (see recipe page 116)
¼ cup (60ml) japanese soy sauce
2 tablespoons mirin
1 teaspoon sugar
1 tablespoon vegetable oil
400g (12½ ounces) chicken breast fillets, sliced thinly
2 medium leeks (700g), sliced thinly
¼ teaspoon seven-spice mix

1 Cook noodles in large saucepan of boiling water until tender; drain.
Cover to keep warm.
2 Bring dashi, 2 tablespoons of the sauce, half the mirin and half
the sugar to the boil in medium saucepan. Remove from heat;
cover to keep warm.
3 Heat oil in medium frying pan; cook chicken and leek, stirring, until
chicken is cooked through. Stir in remaining sauce, mirin and sugar;
bring to the boil.
4 Divide noodles among serving bowls; top with chicken mixture, ladle
over broth. Sprinkle with seven-spice mix.

prep + cook time 35 minutes **serves** 4
nutritional count per serving 11.4g total fat (2.6g saturated fat);
1726kJ (413 cal); 41.1g carbohydrate; 32.1g protein; 4.7g fibre
tip You could add 1 tablespoon grated fresh ginger to the broth for extra
flavour, if you like.

Tempura udon

320g (10 ounces) dried thick udon noodles
1 litre (4 cups) primary dashi (see recipe page 116)
½ cup (125ml) japanese soy sauce
½ cup (125ml) mirin
8 uncooked large king prawns (shrimp) (560g)
vegetable oil, for deep-frying
plain (all-purpose) flour, for dusting
¼ teaspoon seven-spice mix
2 green onions (scallions), chopped finely
tempura batter
½ cup (75g) plain (all-purpose) flour
½ cup (75g) cornflour (cornstarch)
1 teaspoon baking powder
1 cup (250ml) iced soda water

1 Cook noodles in large saucepan of boiling water until tender; drain.
2 Bring dashi, sauce and mirin to the boil in medium saucepan.
Reduce heat; simmer 10 minutes.
3 Meanwhile, shell and devein prawns, leaving tails intact. Score underside
of prawns to prevent curling during cooking.
4 Make tempura batter.
5 Heat oil in small saucepan. Dip prawns, one at a time, in flour, shake off
excess; dip in tempura batter. Deep-fry until golden; drain on absorbent
paper. Repeat until all prawns are cooked.
6 Just before serving, divide noodles among serving bowls; top with
prawns, ladle over broth. Sprinkle with seven-spice mix and onion.
tempura batter Combine ingredients in medium bowl. Do not overmix;
mixture should be lumpy.

prep + cook time 30 minutes **serves** 4
nutritional count per serving 11.5g total fat (1.7g saturated fat);
2521kJ (603 cal); 87g carbohydrate; 30g protein; 3.5g fibre
tip Always use fresh, clean oil and keep at a constant temperature
during cooking. Optimum temperature for vegetables is fairly hot,
about 170°C/335°F, and for seafood slightly higher.

Mixed one-pot dish

300g (9½ ounces) firm tofu
30g (1 ounce) dried cellophane
   noodles
8 fresh shiitake mushrooms
8 uncooked medium king prawns
   (shrimp) (360g)
8 medium mussels (200g)
200g (6½ ounces) chicken
   breast fillets, cut into 5cm
   (2-inch) pieces
200g (6½ ounces) pork fillet,
   sliced thinly
200g (6½ ounces) firm white
   fish fillets, cut into 5cm
   (2-inch) pieces

8 medium oysters (200g)
8 scallops (320g), roe removed
2 medium carrots (240g),
   sliced thinly lengthways
2 medium leeks (700g),
   sliced thickly
4 wombok (napa cabbage) leaves,
   chopped coarsely
1 litre (4 cups) secondary dashi
   (see recipe page 117)
2 tablespoons japanese soy sauce
2 tablespoons mirin
2 tablespoons sake
4 green onions (scallions),
   chopped finely

1 Press tofu between two chopping boards with weight on top, raise
one end; stand 25 minutes. Cut tofu into 2cm (¾-inch) cubes.
2 Meanwhile, place noodles in medium heatproof bowl, cover with
boiling water, stand until tender; drain.
3 Discard mushroom stems; cut a cross in top of caps. Shell and
devein prawns, leaving tails intact. Scrub mussels; remove beards.
4 Arrange meats, seafood, vegetables and tofu on a large platter.
5 Bring dashi, sauce, mirin and sake to the boil in large flameproof
casserole dish on a portable cooker, or in an electric frying pan,
at the table.
6 Add a selection of ingredients to broth and simmer until just cooked.
Repeat with remaining ingredients. Add extra dashi or water if needed.
Serve with individual serving bowls of onion and mounded red maple
radish (see recipe page 281) in ponzu sauce (see recipe page 273),
if you like.

prep + cook time 30 minutes (+ standing) **serves** 4
nutritional count per serving 12.7g total fat (2.9g saturated fat);
1919kJ (459 cal); 12.5g carbohydrate; 64.6g protein; 11.4g fibre
tip You can use drained gelatinous noodles instead of the cellophane
noodles, if you like.

Fried noodles

250g (8 ounces) dried wheat noodles
2 tablespoons peanut oil
500g (1 pound) pork fillets, sliced thinly
1 large brown onion (200g), sliced thinly
1 medium red capsicum (bell pepper) (200g), sliced thinly
1 medium green capsicum (bell pepper) (200g), sliced thinly
140g (5½ ounces) wombok (napa cabbage), shredded coarsely
¼ cup (60ml) tonkatsu sauce
¼ cup (60ml) sukiyaki sauce

1 Cook noodles in large saucepan of boiling water until tender; drain. Rinse under cold water; drain.
2 Meanwhile, heat half the oil in wok; stir-fry pork, in batches, until browned all over. Remove from wok.
3 Heat remaining oil in wok; stir-fry onion until soft. Add capsicums; stir-fry until tender.
4 Return pork to wok with noodles, cabbage and sauces; stir-fry until cabbage wilts.

prep + cook time 35 minutes **serves** 4
nutritional count per serving 15.9g total fat (3.1g saturated fat); 2153kJ (515 cal); 52.7g carbohydrate; 37.3g protein; 5g fibre
tip You can use soba, fresh hokkien or rice noodles in this dish.

321

Vegetables

Soya bean and asparagus soup with mizuna pesto

650g (1¼ pounds) fresh
soya beans, shelled
20g (¾ ounce) butter
2 teaspoons soya bean oil
1 medium brown onion (150g),
chopped finely
1 stalk celery (150g),
chopped finely
1 bay leaf
1 large potato (300g),
chopped finely
1 litre (4 cups) secondary dashi
(see recipe page 117)
2 tablespoons mirin
170g (5½ ounces) asparagus,
chopped coarsely

mizuna pesto
30g (1 ounce) mizuna leaves
2 tablespoons coarsely chopped
japanese parsley (mitsuba)
2 tablespoons slivered almonds,
roasted
2 tablespoon soya bean oil
1 tablespoon finely grated
parmesan cheese
1 clove garlic
pinch finely chopped lemon rind

1 Drop beans into large saucepan of boiling water, return to the boil; drain. When beans are cool enough to handle, discard outer shells. Reserve ¼ cup beans for serving.
2 Heat butter and oil in medium saucepan; cook onion, celery and leaf, stirring, until onion softens. Add potato, dashi and mirin; bring to the boil. Reduce heat; simmer, uncovered, 10 minutes. Add beans and asparagus; simmer, uncovered, about 5 minutes, or until tender. Discard leaf.
3 Stand soup 10 minutes then blend or process soup until smooth; strain through a fine sieve into large bowl.
4 Meanwhile, make mizuna pesto.
5 Serve soup topped with pesto and reserved beans.
mizuna pesto Blend or process ingredients until smooth.

prep + cook time 40 minutes **serves** 6
nutritional count per serving 21.4g total fat (4.6g saturated fat); 1409kJ (337 cal); 11.8g carbohydrate; 19.9g protein; 10g fibre
tip You can use frozen soya beans, available from Asian groceries, in this recipe if fresh are hard to find. You could also use the same quantity of fresh broad beans or 2 cups of frozen broad beans instead.

Kumara gnocchi with pickled ginger brown butter

2 large kumara (orange sweet potato) (1.2kg)
2½ cups (375g) plain (all-purpose) flour
2 egg yolks
2 tablespoons grated parmesan cheese
2 teaspoons vegetable oil
10 slices pancetta (150g), chopped finely
2 teaspoons olive oil
100g (3 ounces) butter
3 cloves garlic, crushed
⅓ cup (90g) drained pickled ginger, shredded
90g (3 ounces) baby spinach leaves

1 Preheat oven to 200°C/400°F.
2 Pierce kumara all over with fork; place on oven tray. Roast 2 hours until very tender.
3 When kumara are cool enough to handle, peel, then chop coarsely. Using wooden spoon, push through fine sieve or mouli into large bowl. Stir in flour, yolks and cheese. Knead gently on floured surface until mixture comes together. Dough should be soft, pliable and slightly damp but not sticky.
4 Heat vegetable oil in frying pan; cook pancetta until crisp. Drain.
5 Divide dough into four portions. Roll each portion into 2cm (¾-inch) thick log, then cut into 2cm (¾-inch) lengths with sharp knife.
6 Cook gnocchi, in batches, in large saucepan of boiling water about 2 minutes or until gnocchi float to surface. Remove gnocchi from pan with slotted spoon; drain. Gently toss gnocchi in large bowl with olive oil.
7 Meanwhile, melt butter in medium saucepan, stirring, about 3 minutes or until butter foams then turns golden. Stir in garlic and ginger; remove pan from heat. Add to gnocchi with baby spinach and pancetta; toss gently to combine. Sprinkle with extra pickled ginger, if you like.

prep + cook time 3 hours (+ cooling) **serves** 4
nutritional count per serving 35.7g total fat (17.8g saturated fat); 3616kJ (865 cal); 105g carbohydrate; 26g protein; 9.6g fibre
tip Do not overwork the dough or it will toughen.

327

Soya beans and vegetables

2¼ cups (450g) dried soya beans
10cm (4-inch) piece kelp (konbu)
2 cloves garlic, bruised
3 bay leaves
¼ cup (60ml) olive oil
40g (1½ ounces) butter
2 large onions (400g), chopped
3 medium carrots (360g), chopped
2 stalks celery (300g), chopped
½ small daikon (250g), chopped
3 baby eggplants (180g), chopped
125g (4 ounces) burdock root,
   peeled, shaved
1½ tablespoons plain
   (all-purpose) flour

¾ cup (185ml) mirin
½ cup (125ml) sake
3 cups (750ml) vegetable stock
400g (12½-ounce) can diced
   tomatoes
2 tablespoons red miso
2 tablespoons japanese soy sauce
1 tablespoon chopped fresh thyme
2cm (¾-inch) piece fresh ginger
   (10g), grated
1 teaspoon finely grated lemon rind
1½ cups (90g) japanese
   breadcrumbs
2 tablespoons chopped finely
   flat-leaf parsley

1 Soak beans and kelp in cold water overnight; drain. Discard kelp.
2 Place beans, garlic and 2 of the bay leaves in large saucepan with
enough water to cover; bring to the boil. Reduce heat; simmer 2½ hours
or until tender. Drain. Rinse under cold water; drain.
3 Preheat oven to 180°C/350°F.
4 Heat half the oil and half the butter with remaining bay leaf in large
saucepan; cook onion, stirring, 15 minutes. Remove from pan.
5 Add a little more oil to pan; cook carrot, celery and daikon, stirring
occasionally, 15 minutes or until golden. Remove from pan.
6 Add remaining oil; cook eggplant and burdock, 5 minutes. Remove
from pan.
7 Melt remaining butter in pan; cook flour, stirring, 1 minute. Whisk in
mirin and sake until smooth. Stir in stock, tomato, miso, sauce, thyme,
ginger and rind. Bring to the boil, then simmer until slightly thickened.
8 Place beans, vegetables and sauce in 5-litre (20-cup) ovenproof dish;
bake, covered, 2 hours. Sprinkle with breadcrumbs and parsley; bake,
uncovered, further 30 minutes or until golden. Serve with japanese
mayonnaise, if you like.

prep + cook time 5 hours 30 minutes (+ standing) **serves** 8
nutritional count per serving 23.9g total fat (5.7g saturated fat);
1969kJ (471 cal); 24.9g carbohydrate; 23.7g protein; 16.5g fibre

Vegetarian sukiyaki

350g (11 ounces) firm tofu
440g (14 ounces) fresh udon noodles
8 fresh shiitake mushrooms
4 green onions (scallions), cut into chunks
100g (3 ounces) baby spinach leaves
230g (7 ounces) can bamboo shoots, drained
350g (11 ounces) wombok (napa cabbage), chopped coarsely
100g (3 ounces) enoki mushrooms, trimmed
1 small leek (200g), chopped coarsely
2 medium carrots (240g), sliced thickly
4 eggs
broth
1 cup (250ml) japanese soy sauce
½ cup (125ml) sake
½ cup (125ml) mirin
1 cup (250ml) water
½ cup (110g) sugar

1 Press tofu between two chopping boards with weight on top, raise one end; stand 25 minutes. Cut into 2cm (¾-inch) cubes.
2 Rinse noodles under hot water; drain. Cut into random lengths.
3 Make broth.
4 Meanwhile, remove and discard shiitake stems; cut a cross in top of caps.
5 Arrange all ingredients, except eggs, on serving platters or in bowls. Place broth in medium bowl.
6 Break eggs into individual bowls; beat lightly.
7 Pour broth into sukiyaki pan (or electric frying pan). Heat pan on portable gas cooker at the table; cook a quarter of the noodles and a quarter of the remaining ingredients in broth, uncovered, until just tender. Dip cooked ingredients into egg before eating. Repeat process until all the remaining noodles and ingredients are cooked.
broth Stir ingredients in medium saucepan over heat until sugar dissolves.

prep + cook time 30 minutes **serves** 4
nutritional count per serving 11.9g total fat (2.5g saturated fat); 2232kJ (534 cal); 65.8g carbohydrate; 29g protein; 9.4g fibre
tip A traditional sukiyaki pan is available from Japanese stores.

Vegetable tempura

250g (8 ounces) firm tofu
1 medium brown onion (150g)
1 small fresh or frozen
  lotus root (200g)
8 fresh shiitake mushrooms
2 sheets toasted seaweed
  (yaki-nori)
20g (¾ ounce) cellophane
  noodles, cut in half
vegetable oil, for deep-frying
plain flour, for dusting
120g (4 ounces) pumpkin, sliced
50g (1½ ounces) green beans,
  halved

1 small kumara (orange sweet
  potato) (250g), sliced thinly
1 baby eggplant (60g), sliced
1 small red capsicum (bell pepper)
  (150g), seeded, cut into squares
1 medium carrot (120g), sliced
1 medium lemon (140g),
  cut into wedges
batter
1 egg, beaten lightly
2 cups (500ml) iced soda water
1 cup (150g) plain (all-purpose)
  flour
1 cup (150g) cornflour (cornstarch)

1 Press tofu between two chopping boards with weight on top, raise
one end; stand 25 minutes. Cut into 2cm (¾-inch) cubes.
2 Halve onion from root end. Insert toothpicks at regular intervals to hold
onion rings together and slice in between.
3 Peel lotus root and slice; place in water with a dash of vinegar to prevent
browning. (If using canned lotus, drain and slice.) Discard mushroom
stems; cut a cross in top of caps.
4 Cut one sheet nori into 5cm (2-inch) squares; halve other sheet, cut
into 2cm (¾-inch) wide strips. Brush nori strips with water, wrap tightly
around middle of 10 noodles; reserve noodle bunches.
5 Make batter.
6 Heat oil in large saucepan. Dust ingredients, except nori squares,
lightly in flour; shake off excess. Dip nori squares and other ingredients
in batter, drain excess; deep-fry, in batches, until golden. Drain. Only fry in
small batches and ensure oil comes back to correct temperature before
adding next batch. Deep-fry noodle bundles.
7 Serve tempura and noodles immediately with lemon and tempura
dipping sauce (see recipe page 15) with a little grated daikon, if you like.
batter Combine egg and soda water in bowl. Add sifted flours at once;
mix lightly until just combined. Do not overmix; mixture should be lumpy.

prep + cook time 40 minutes **serves** 4
nutritional count per serving 39.6g total fat (5.7g saturated fat);
3285kJ (786 cal); 78.3g carbohydrate; 20.3g protein; 11.7g fibre

Sides

Green beans with black sesame sauce

200g (6½ ounces) green beans
⅓ cup (50g) black sesame seeds, toasted
1 tablespoon caster (superfine) sugar
1 tablespoon japanese soy sauce
2 teaspoons mirin

1 Cut beans in half lengthways, then in half widthways. Cook in
saucepan of boiling, salted water for 2 minutes. Drain, then refresh
in iced water. Drain; pat dry with absorbent paper.
2 Blend, process or grind seeds using mortar and pestle until coarse.
Transfer to medium bowl; stir in sugar, sauce and mirin until combined.
Add green beans; toss to coat.

prep + cook time 20 minutes **serves** 4
nutritional count per serving 7.1g total fat (0.9g saturated fat);
451kJ (108 cal); 5.7g carbohydrate; 4.2g protein; 2.6g fibre

Shiitake mushrooms with ponzu sauce

200g (6½ ounces) fresh shiitake mushrooms
1 tablespoon vegetable oil
¼ cup (60ml) ponzu sauce
sesame oil, for serving (optional)

1 Discard stems; halve any large caps.
2 Heat oil in medium frying pan; cook mushrooms until tender.
3 Transfer to shallow bowl; pour over ponzu sauce. Drizzle with a little sesame oil, if you like.

prep + cook time 10 minutes **serves** 4
nutritional count per serving 6.3g total fat (0.8g saturated fat); 322kJ (77 cal); 2.7g carbohydrate; 2g protein; 1.4g fibre
tip Ponzu is a citrus-based sauce and is often used for dipping in Japan. It is readily available from Asian food stores and some major supermarkets, but you can easily make your own (see recipe page 273).

Pumpkin with pickled plum dressing

500g (1 pound) pumpkin, unpeeled, seeded
1 japanese mint (shiso) leaf, shredded finely
pickled plum dressing
2 tablespoons secondary dashi (see recipe page 117)
1 tablespoon mirin
2 teaspoons pickled plum puree
2 teaspoons japanese soy sauce
¼ teaspoon caster (superfine) sugar

1 Cut pumpkin into 2cm (¾-inch) cubes. Peel around edges of skin, leaving small patch of skin on each cube. Run vegetable peeler along sharp edges to slightly round cube shape. Boil, steam or microwave pumpkin until tender. Drain; cool.
2 Meanwhile, make pickled plum dressing.
3 Lightly toss pumpkin with dressing. Serve sprinkled with shiso.
pickled plum dressing Combine ingredients in small bowl.

prep + cook time 30 minutes **serves** 4
nutritional count per serving 0.5g total fat (0.3g saturated fat);
222kJ (53 cal); 8.5g carbohydrate; 2.4g protein; 1.2g fibre
tips Use a combination of basil and mint leaves if you cannot find any japanese mint (shiso).
You will need half a small jap pumpkin for this recipe.

Somen noodle, prawn and cucumber salad

2 lebanese cucumbers (260g)
2 teaspoons salt
1 tablespoon dried seaweed (wakame)
12 cooked medium king prawns (shrimp) (540g)
100g (3 ounces) dried somen noodles
3 green onions (scallions), sliced thinly

ginger dressing
½ teaspoon dashi granules
1 tablespoon hot water
½ cup (125ml) rice vinegar
¼ cup (60ml) mirin
1 teaspoon japanese soy sauce
½ teaspoon sesame oil
2cm (¾-inch) piece fresh ginger (10g), grated
pinch caster (superfine) sugar

1 Halve cucumber lengthways; discard seeds with teaspoon. Slice thinly on diagonal; place in colander. Sprinkle with salt; stand 10 minutes. Rinse under cold water; drain, gently squeezing out excess moisture. Refrigerate.
2 Meanwhile, make ginger dressing.
3 Place seaweed in small bowl, cover with cold water, stand 5 minutes; drain.
4 Shell and devein prawns; halve lengthways.
5 Cook noodles in large saucepan of boiling water until tender; drain. Rinse under cold water; drain.
6 Place cucumber, seaweed, prawns in large bowl with dressing and half the onion; toss gently to combine. Serve sprinkled with remaining onion and a little seven-spice mix, if you like.
ginger dressing Dissolve granules in the water in small bowl. Stir in remaining ingredients; chill.

prep + cook time 30 minutes **serves** 4
nutritional count per serving 1.7g total fat (0.3g saturated fat); 769kJ (184 cal); 18.5g carbohydrate; 19.3g protein; 1.6g fibre

Grilled corn

3 corn cobs, husk removed (750g), halved
30g (1 ounce) butter, melted
3 teaspoons japanese soy sauce
2 teaspoons mirin
1 teaspoon caster (superfine) sugar

1 Boil, steam or microwave corn until tender; drain.
2 Place cobs on foil-lined-oven tray.
3 Preheat grill.
4 Combine butter, sauce, mirin and sugar in small bowl; brush over corn.
Roast corn under grill about 5 minutes, turning and basting regularly
with butter mixture. Brush any remaining butter mixture over corn
before serving.

prep + cook time 15 minutes **serves** 4
nutritional count per serving 7.8g total fat (4.2g saturated fat);
849kJ (203 cal); 23.7g carbohydrate; 6g protein; 6.2g fibre

Roast pumpkin and ginger mash

1.5kg (3 pounds) pumpkin
1 tablespoon vegetable oil
100g (3 ounces) butter, diced
¼ teaspoon sesame oil
2 teaspoons japanese soy sauce
2cm (¾-inch) piece fresh ginger (10g), grated

1 Preheat oven to 220°C/425°F.
2 Seed and cut pumpkin into chunks. Place pumpkin, skin-side down, on oven tray; drizzle with vegetable oil. Roast 1 hour 20 minutes or until tender. Stand 10 minutes. Discard skin.
3 Mash pumpkin with butter and sesame oil until smooth. Stir in sauce and ginger.

prep + cook time 1 hour 40 minutes **serves** 6
nutritional count per serving 17.7g total fat (10g saturated fat); 974kJ (233 cal); 13.3g carbohydrate; 4.5g protein; 2.5g fibre

Honey soy roasted vegetables

1 medium white kumara (sweet potato) (400g)
1 small orange kumara (sweet potato) (250g)
1 large potato (300g)
1 medium daikon (600g)
450g (14½ ounces) pumpkin, seeded
¼ cup (60ml) vegetable oil
1 teaspoon sesame oil
1½ tablespoons honey
1 tablespoon white sesame seeds
10g (½ ounce) butter
3 teaspoons japanese soy sauce

1 Preheat oven to 200°C/400°F.
2 Peel vegetables except pumpkin; cut into chunks. Place pumpkin on oven tray in single layer; place remaining vegetables on another oven tray in single layer. Drizzle both trays with combined oils. Roast 45 minutes or until golden and tender, shaking trays occasionally. (Pumpkin will be cooked before other vegetables. Remove pumpkin after 30 minutes.)
3 Meanwhile, stir honey, seeds, butter and sauce in small saucepan over heat until combined.
4 Combine roasted vegetables on one tray; drizzle over honey mixture. Roast another 10 minutes, shaking tray occasionally, until vegetables are glazed and sesame seeds toasted.

prep + cook time 1 hour 25 minutes **serves** 6
nutritional count per serving 13g total fat (2.5g saturated fat); 1154kJ (276 cal); 32.8g carbohydrate; 5g protein; 4.9g fibre
tip If white kumara is difficult to find, use parsnip instead.

Daikon and potato gratin

3 medium potatoes (500g), sliced thinly
1 large daikon (800g), sliced thinly
1½ tablespoons salt
2½ cups (625ml) pouring cream
10cm (4-inch) piece of kelp (konbu)
3 spring onions (75g), chopped finely
2 bay leaves
2 cloves garlic, crushed

1 Place potato in medium bowl covered with cold water. Place daikon in colander, sprinkle with salt; stand 45 minutes.
2 Meanwhile, bring cream, konbu, onion, leaves and garlic to the boil in large saucepan; discard konbu. Reduce heat; simmer, uncovered, 2 minutes. Discard leaves; season with salt and white pepper.
3 Rinse daikon under cold water; drain, gently squeezing out excess moisture. Drain potato. Pat vegetables dry with absorbent paper.
4 Preheat oven to 200°C/400°F. Grease 2-litre (8-cup) ovenproof dish.
5 Layer vegetable slices in dish, pouring some of the cream mixture between each layer; pour any remaining cream mixture over the top.
6 Bake gratin, covered with foil, 50 minutes. Remove foil; bake further 20 minutes or until top is bubbling and golden. Stand gratin 10 minutes before serving.

prep + cook time 2 hours 20 minutes (+ standing) **serves** 8
nutritional count per serving 32.8g total fat (21.4g saturated fat); 1492kJ (357 cal); 11.9g carbohydrate; 3.5g protein; 2.6g fibre
tips Use a mandoline to slice potato and daikon into very thin rounds. Don't be tempted to skip the salting process as this draws the excess liquid from the daikon. You may end up with a watery dish otherwise. You can use 600ml carton of cream without affecting the recipe.

Simmered green beans

250g (8 ounces) green beans, trimmed, halved
1½ cups (375ml) primary dashi (see recipe page 116)
2 tablespoons japanese soy sauce
2 tablespoons sake
2 teaspoons smoked dried bonito flakes

1 Bring beans, dashi, sauce and sake to the boil in medium saucepan. Reduce heat; simmer, uncovered, until beans are just tender. Drain over small bowl; reserve liquid.
2 Arrange beans in individual bowls; pour over a little of the reserved liquid. Serve either hot, at room temperature, or chilled, sprinkle with bonito flakes.

prep + cook time 10 minutes **serves** 4
nutritional count per serving 0.4g total fat (0.1g saturated fat); 155kJ (37 cal); 2.5g carbohydrate; 3.1g protein; 1.7g fibre
tips This dish will keep for 2 or 3 days in the refrigerator.
Bonito is an oily fish which, when dried and flaked, is widely used in the Japanese kitchen. You could serve the beans with japanese mustard instead of the bonito and use dry white wine instead of sake.

Spinach with
roasted sesame seed dressing

⅓ cup (50g) white sesame seeds, toasted
¼ cup (60ml) primary dashi (see recipe page 116)
1½ tablespoons japanese soy sauce
1 teaspoon sugar
600g (1¼ pounds) spinach, trimmed

1 Reserve 1 teaspoon of the seeds; blend, process or grind remaining seeds until smooth.
2 Place ground seeds with dashi, sauce and sugar in screw-top jar; shake until sugar dissolves.
3 Cook spinach in medium saucepan of boiling water for 30 seconds; drain immediately. Rinse under cold running water. Wrap spinach in bamboo mat, roll firmly and gently squeeze out excess water; place on serving plate.
4 Just before serving, pour dressing over spinach. Serve at room temperature, sprinkled with reserved seeds.

prep + cook time 20 minutes **serves** 4
nutritional count per serving 7.2g total fat (0.9g saturated fat); 418kJ (100 cal); 1.9g carbohydrate; 5.3g protein; 3.4g fibre
tips You could use tahini (sesame seed paste) instead of grinding the toasted sesame seeds.
Beans or watercress can be used instead of spinach in this salad, and peanuts or macadamia nuts could be substituted for the sesame seeds. If you like, you can sprinkle the cooked spinach with smoked dried bonito flakes.

Sweet soy pumpkin

500g (1 pound) pumpkin, unpeeled, seeded
1½ cups (375ml) secondary dashi (see recipe page 117)
2 tablespoons mirin
1½ tablespoons sugar
1 tablespoon japanese soy sauce

1 Cut pumpkin into chunks; slice skin off at random to give surface a mottled appearance.
2 Place pumpkin in medium saucepan, skin-side down; add dashi, mirin and sugar. Bring to the boil. Reduce heat; simmer, covered, 5 minutes, turning pumpkin pieces after 2 minutes.
3 Add sauce; cook 8 minutes or until pumpkin is tender, turning pieces halfway through. Remove from heat; stand 5 minutes.
4 Serve pumpkin hot or at room temperature drizzled with cooking liquid.

prep + cook time 25 minutes (+ cooling) **serve** 4
nutritional count per serving 0.6g total fat (0.4g saturated fat); 343kJ (82 cal); 13.8g carbohydrate; 3.5g protein; 1.2g fibre
tip You will need half a small jap pumpkin to make this recipe.

Tofu and avocado dressing

150g (5 ounces) silken firm tofu
1 small avocado (200g)
½ teaspoon lemon juice
¼ cup (50g) cottage cheese
2 tablespoons mayonnaise
1½ teaspoons chicken stock powder

1 Press tofu between two chopping boards with weight on top,
raise one end; stand 25 minutes.
2 Mash avocado with juice until smooth. Cut tofu into chunks,
add to avocado mixture with cottage cheese; whisk until combined.
Whisk in mayonnaise and powder. Season to taste.

prep time 10 minutes (+ standing) **makes** 1½ cups
nutritional count per tablespoon 3.3g total fat (0.7g saturated fat);
163kJ (39 cal); 0.6g carbohydrate; 1.6g protein; 0.7g fibre
tips It is important to use silken tofu for this recipe to get the right texture.
This recipe makes a good accompaniment to deep-fried fish or grilled
chicken pieces.

Tempura salt and pepper potatoes with mirin dressing

1 cup (150g) rice flour
1¾ cups (255g) cornflour
  (cornstarch)
1¼ cups (310ml) chilled
  soda water
500g (1 pound) bintje potatoes,
  peeled
vegetable oil, for deep-frying
roasted salt and pepper spice
1 tablespoon sea salt flakes
2 cinnamon sticks
4 star anise
½ teaspoon japanese pepper

mirin dressing
1 clove garlic, crushed
4cm (1½-inch) piece fresh ginger
  (20g), chopped finely
2 fresh small red thai chillies
  (serrano chilies), sliced thinly
½ cup (125ml) water
¼ cup (60ml) japanese soy sauce
¼ cup (55g) sugar
¼ cup (60ml) mirin
1½ tablespoons rice wine vinegar

1 Place rice flour and 1 cup of the cornflour in medium bowl; stir in soda water until just combined (batter should be lumpy). Cover; stand 30 minutes.
2 Make roasted salt and pepper spice and mirin dressing.
3 Using sharp knife, mandoline or V-slicer, slice potato thinly; pat dry with absorbent paper.
4 Heat oil in large saucepan. Dust potato slices, one at a time, with remaining cornflour, then dip in batter; deep-fry potato, in batches, until golden and tender. Drain on absorbent paper. Sprinkle with roasted salt and pepper spice and serve with mirin dressing.
roasted salt and pepper spice Preheat oven to 150°C/300°F. Roast salt, cinnamon and star anise on oven tray for 1 hour. Blend, process or grind spices with pepper until powdered. Push spice mixture through fine sieve into small bowl.
mirin dressing Bring ingredients to the boil in small saucepan. Reduce heat; simmer, uncovered, 5 minutes.

prep + cook time 1 hour 30 minutes (+ standing) **serves** 4
nutritional count per serving 16.7g total fat (2.2g saturated fat); 2675kJ (640 cal); 112.3g carbohydrate; 5.8g protein; 2.7g fibre

Marinated mixed mushrooms

200g (6½ ounces) oyster mushrooms
200g (6½ ounces) shiitake mushrooms
200g (6½ ounces) button mushrooms
200g (6½ ounces) swiss brown mushrooms
200g (6½ ounces) enoki mushrooms
2 cloves garlic, crushed
4cm (1½-inch) piece fresh ginger (20g), grated
⅓ cup (80ml) light soy sauce
2 tablespoons mirin
2 tablespoons sake
2 tablespoons peanut oil
1 tablespoon sugar
4 green onions (scallions), sliced thickly

1 Combine mushrooms, garlic, ginger, sauce, mirin, sake, oil and sugar in large bowl. Cover; refrigerate 2 hours.

2 Drain mushrooms over small bowl; reserve marinade.

3 Cook mushrooms on heated oiled grill plate (or grill or barbecue) until tender.

4 Place mushrooms in medium bowl with onion and reserved marinade; toss gently to coat.

prep + cook time 25 minutes (+ refrigeration) **serves** 4
nutritional count per serving 9.8g total fat (1.7g saturated fat); 890kJ (213 cal); 14.9g carbohydrate; 9.2g protein; 7.7g fibre

Desserts

Sweet fritters

1 egg
½ cup (125ml) evaporated milk
⅓ cup (95g) sweet red bean paste
1 cup (150g) self-raising flour
⅓ cup (75g) firmly packed light brown sugar
¼ teaspoon ground cinnamon
pinch of salt
peanut oil, for deep-frying
¼ cup (55g) caster (superfine) sugar

1 Combine egg, milk and paste in small jug.
2 Combine flour, brown sugar, cinnamon and salt in medium bowl;
stir in egg mixture until combined.
3 Heat oil in large saucepan; deep-fry tablespoons of batter, in batches,
on low heat about 5 minutes or until golden and cooked through.
Drain on absorbent paper.
4 Roll hot fritters in caster sugar to coat. Serve immediately.

prep + cook time 20 minutes **makes** 20
nutritional count per fritter 2.3g total fat (0.7g saturated fat);
288kJ (69 cal); 10.5g carbohydrate; 1.7g protein; 0.5g fibre

Nashi and ginger strudel

4 medium nashi pears (800g)
1 tablespoon lemon juice
1cm (½-inch) piece fresh ginger (5g), grated
½ cup (30g) japanese breadcrumbs
¾ cup (165g) caster (superfine) sugar
¼ cup (35g) white sesame seeds, toasted
½ cup (60g) walnuts, chopped finely
1 teaspoon ground ginger
1½ teaspoons ground cinnamon
8 sheets fillo pastry
150g (5½ ounces) unsalted butter, melted
2 tablespoons pure icing (confectioner's) sugar

1 Preheat oven to 180°C/350°F. Grease oven tray.
2 Peel, core and slice pear thickly. Place pear, juice, fresh ginger, breadcrumbs and ¼ cup of the caster sugar in large bowl.
3 Combine seeds, walnuts, spices and remaining caster sugar in small bowl.
4 Lay one sheet of pastry on work bench, long edge towards you; brush with butter. Lay another sheet of pastry on top so it overlaps edge furthest away from you by 5cm (2 inches); brush with butter. Sprinkle one-quarter of the seed mixture over pastry. Repeat layering with pastry and seed mixture, brushing each sheet of pastry with butter.
5 Spoon pear filling along edge closest to you, leaving 5cm (2-inch) border along edge of pastry closest to you and on both sides. Fold short sides of pastry over filling; roll strudel away from you to enclose filling and form log. Place strudel on tray, seam-side down; brush with butter.
6 Bake strudel about 50 minutes or until browned. Serve dusted with icing sugar.

prep + cook time 1 hour 15 minutes **serves** 12
nutritional count per serving 5.9g total fat (7.3g saturated fat); 1141kJ (273 cal); 29.7g carbohydrate; 3.2g protein; 1.8g fibre

Chocolate pudding with red bean heart

1 tablespoon sweet red bean paste
150g (5½ ounces) dark cooking chocolate, chopped
125g (4 ounces) unsalted butter, chopped
½ cup (75g) plain (all-purpose) flour
¼ cup (35g) self-raising flour
⅓ cup (75g) caster (superfine) sugar
4 eggs, beaten lightly
1 teaspoon cocoa powder

1 Preheat oven to 200°C/400°F. Grease six ½-cup (125ml) ovenproof dishes.
2 Place bean paste and 25g (¾ ounce) of the chocolate in small heatproof bowl over small saucepan of simmering water (do not allow water to touch base of bowl); stir until melted. Cover; refrigerate 2 hours or until firm.
3 Place remaining chocolate and butter in medium heatproof bowl over medium saucepan of simmering water (do not allow water to touch base of bowl); stir until melted.
4 Combine flours, sugar and egg in another medium bowl. Stir in butter mixture until smooth. Cover; refrigerate 30 minutes.
5 Spoon three-quarters of the pudding mixture among dishes. Drop 1 teaspoon of chocolate bean mixture into centre of each pudding; top with remaining pudding mixture.
6 Bake puddings about 13 minutes. Stand puddings in dishes 2 minutes; turn onto serving plates, dust with cocoa.

prep + cook time 35 minutes (+ refrigeration & standing) **serves** 6
nutritional count per serving 28.8g total fat (16.9g saturated fat); 1910kJ (457 cal); 42.2g carbohydrate; 8.8g protein; 1.3g fibre

Banana tempura

1 egg
¾ cup (185ml) iced water
⅔ cup (100g) tempura flour
vegetable oil, for deep-frying
4 small bananas (520g)
1 tablespoon caster (superfine) sugar

1 Combine egg and the water in medium bowl; mix in flour until just combined, but still lumpy.
2 Heat oil in large saucepan.
3 Halve bananas lengthways. Working in batches, dip banana in batter; deep-fry bananas until crisp and golden. Drain on absorbent paper; sprinkle with sugar.
4 Serve bananas immediately, with green tea ice-cream (see recipe page 374), if you like.

prep + cook time 15 minutes **serves** 4
nutritional count per serving 11.6g total fat (1.7g saturated fat); 1212kJ (290 cal); 39.6g carbohydrate; 6.1g protein; 2.9g fibre

Green tea ice-cream

1 vanilla bean
2½ cups (625ml) thickened (heavy) cream
1 cup (250ml) milk
9 egg yolks
⅔ cup (150g) caster (superfine) sugar
1 tablespoon green tea powder

1 Split vanilla bean lengthways; scrape out seeds. Stir pod, seeds, cream and milk in medium saucepan over heat until almost boiling. Remove from heat; stand 15 minutes.
2 Beat egg yolks and sugar in medium bowl with electric mixer until thick and creamy. Whisking constantly, gradually add cream mixture to egg mixture until smooth. Return to clean pan; stir over low heat, without boiling, about 10 minutes or until sauce thickens and coats back of wooden spoon.
3 Blend powder and 2 tablespoons of the custard mixture in small bowl until smooth; whisk into custard until smooth.
4 Strain custard into large bowl; discard pods. Cool 10 minutes. Cover surface of custard with plastic wrap; refrigerate until cold.
5 Pour custard into ice-cream maker, churn according to manufacturer's instructions.

prep + cook time 25 minutes (+ standing, refrigeration & churning)
serves 8
nutritional count per serving 35.9g total fat (21.6g saturated fat); 1797kJ (430 cal); 23g carbohydrate; 5.9g protein; 0g fibre
tips Green tea powder is available from Asian food stores.
If you don't have an ice-cream maker, pour custard into shallow container and cover with foil; freeze until almost firm. Place ice-cream in large bowl, chop coarsely then beat with electric mixer until smooth. Pour into deep container; cover, freeze until firm. Repeat process twice more.

Plum granita

½ cup (110g) caster (superfine) sugar
2 strips lemon rind
1½ cups (375ml) water
825g (1¾ pounds) can whole plums in juice
¼ cup (60ml) sake

1 Stir sugar, rind and the water in medium saucepan over heat, without boiling, until sugar dissolves. Bring to the boil. Reduce heat; simmer, uncovered, 10 minutes. Refrigerate until cold; discard rind.
2 Meanwhile, drain plums over medium bowl; reserve juice. Halve plums, discard stones. Process plums until smooth; strain into medium bowl.
3 Combine cooled syrup, pureed plum juice, reserved juices and sake in shallow 30cm x 20cm (12-inch x 8-inch) metallic container; freeze 1 hour. Scrape frozen edges back into mixture with fork. Return to freezer; repeat another three times until mixture resembles crushed ice. Freeze until ready to serve.
4 Just before serving, beat mixture with fork.

prep + cook time 25 minutes (+ refrigeration & freezing) **serves** 8
nutritional count per serving 0g total fat (0g saturated fat); 506kJ (121 cal); 28.4g carbohydrate; 0.5g protein; 1.1g fibre
tip For a refreshing summer cocktail, serve plum granita in martini glasses topped with sparkling wine.

Rockmelon and lychees with citrus syrup

½ vanilla bean
¾ cup (180ml) water
⅓ cup (75g) caster (superfine) sugar
1 teaspoon grated lemon rind
1 teaspoon grated lime rind
1 rockmelon (1kg)
15 fresh lychees (375g)

1 Split vanilla bean lengthways; scrape out seeds. Stir pod, seeds, the water, sugar and rinds in small saucepan over medium heat, without boiling, until sugar dissolves; bring to the boil. Boil, uncovered, without stirring, 8 minutes or until syrupy. Cool to room temperature; discard pod.
2 Meanwhile, peel and seed rockmelon; cut into chunks. Peel and stone lychees.
3 Place fruit in large bowl with syrup; toss gently to combine. Refrigerate until cold.

prep + cook time 20 minutes (+ refrigeration) **serves** 4
nutritional count per serving 0.2g total fat (0g saturated fat); 681kJ (163 cal); 38.4g carbohydrate; 1.7g protein; 2.7g fibre

Green tea pots with baked rhubarb

1½ teaspoons green tea powder
2½ cups (625ml) pouring cream
¾ cup (165g) caster (superfine) sugar
3 teaspoons gelatine
½ cup (125ml) milk
½ teaspoon vanilla extract
baked rhubarb
6 large stems (200g) trimmed rhubarb, cut into chunks
⅓ cup (75g) caster (superfine) sugar
25g (¾ ounce) unsalted butter, diced

1 Blend powder and 2 tablespoons of the cream in medium saucepan until smooth; whisk in remaining cream. Add sugar; stir over heat, without boiling, until sugar dissolves. Sprinkle gelatine over cream mixture; stir over heat, without boiling, until gelatine dissolves. Remove pan from heat; stand 10 minutes.
2 Strain cream mixture into medium jug; stir in milk and extract. Pour mixture into eight ½-cup (125ml) dishes. Refrigerate 3 hours or until set.
3 Meanwhile, make baked rhubarb.
4 Serve green tea pots topped with rhubarb.
baked rhubarb Preheat oven to 220°C/425°F. Place rhubarb, in single layer, in large baking dish. Sprinkle with sugar; dot with butter. Bake about 15 minutes or until rhubarb is tender but still holds its shape. Cool to room temperature.

prep + cook time 20 minutes (+ standing & refrigeration) **serves** 8
nutritional count per serving 37.1g total fat (24.5g saturated fat); 1977kJ (473 cal); 33.6g carbohydrate; 3.5g protein; 0.6g fibre
tip Green tea powder is available from Asian food stores.

Toasted sesame semi-freddo

4 eggs, separated
⅓ cup (55g) pure icing (confectioner's) sugar
¼ cup (80g) honey
¼ cup (30g) roasted soya bean flour
½ cup (75g) white sesame seeds, toasted, crushed lightly
1¼ cups (310ml) thickened (heavy) cream, whipped
3 medium bananas (600g), sliced

1 Line 10cm x 21cm (4-inch x 8-inch) loaf pan with plastic wrap, extending plastic 6cm (2½ inches) over long sides.
2 Beat egg yolks, sugar and 2 tablespoons of the honey in medium bowl with electric mixer until pale and doubled in volume. Stir in flour and seeds; fold in whipped cream.
3 Beat egg whites in small bowl with electric mixer until firm peaks form. Fold one-third egg white through egg yolk mixture, then remaining egg whites. Spoon mixture into pan; cover surface with plastic wrap. Freeze until firm.
4 Serve semi-freddo sliced and topped with banana; drizzle with remaining honey.

prep time 20 minutes (+ freezing) **serves** 8
nutritional count per serving 22.9g total fat (11.1g saturated fat); 1467kJ (351 cal); 27.3g carbohydrate; 9.3g protein; 2.6g fibre
tips Roasted soya bean flour (kinako) is made from ground roasted soya beans. It has a slightly sweet, nutty flavour.
You can use 300ml carton of cream without affecting the recipe.
Remove from freezer 10 minutes before serving to soften slightly.

Steamed vanilla custard cups

4 eggs
2 cups (500ml) pouring cream
1 teaspoon vanilla extract
⅓ cup (75g) caster (superfine) sugar
2 tablespoons sake
½ teaspoon finely grated lemon rind
2 teaspoons caster (superfine) sugar, extra
250g (8 ounces) blueberries

1 Whisk eggs in medium bowl until combined; stir in cream, extract and sugar. Strain mixture into jug; stand 10 minutes.
2 Pour mixture into six 1-cup (250ml) heatproof dishes. Place dishes in large bamboo steamer; place steamer, covered, over large saucepan of simmering water. Cook 30 minutes or until just set. Remove dishes from steamer; cool slightly.
3 Meanwhile, heat sake, rind and extra sugar in small saucepan; bring to the boil. Reduce heat; simmer, uncovered, 1 minute or until syrupy. Add blueberries; simmer, covered, 2 minutes or until syrup turns purple. Remove pan from heat.
4 Serve custards topped with blueberries.

prep + cook time 40 minutes (+ standing & cooling) **serves** 6
nutritional count per serving 43.2g total fat (26g saturated fat); 2094kJ (501 cal); 20.7g carbohydrate; 8.7g protein; 0.9g fibre
tips Wrap the steamer lid in a clean tea towel to avoid condensation drops falling onto the custards.
Cook custards in two batches if they don't all fit in your steamer.

glossary

almonds

blanched almonds with brown skins removed.

flaked paper-thin slices.

ground also known as almond meal.

slivered small pieces cut lengthways.

baking powder a raising agent; two parts cream of tartar to one part bicarbonate of soda (baking soda).

bamboo shoots fibrous shoots; usually available in cans but sometimes fresh.

beans

broad also called fava beans; available dried, fresh, canned and frozen. Fresh beans should be peeled twice — the outer green pod and beige-green inner shell.

snake long (40cm), thin, round, fresh Asian green beans.

soya the most nutritious legume; high in protein and low in carbohydrate.

sprouts new growths of beans and seeds germinated for consumption as sprouts.

bicarbonate of soda also called baking soda.

bonito flakes dried bonito shaved into flakes and packed in cellophane; larger, coarser flakes are used to make dashi while the finer shavings are used as a garnish. Store in an airtight container after opening.

breadcrumbs, japanese (panko) available in two kinds: larger pieces and fine crumbs — have a lighter texture than Western-style breadcrumbs

buk choy also called bok choy, pak choi, chinese white cabbage or chinese chard; has a fresh, mild mustard taste. Use stems and leaves, stir-fried or braised.

butter we use salted butter; 125g is equal to 1 stick (4 ounces).

capsicum also called bell pepper.

cheese

cream commonly called philadelphia or philly cheese; a soft cow's-milk cheese with a fat content of 14–33%.

mozzarella soft, spun-curd cheese generally made from cow's milk.

parmesan also called parmigiano; is a hard, grainy cow's-milk cheese originating in the Parma region of Italy.

cornflour also called cornstarch. Made from corn or wheat.

cream we use fresh pouring cream, also called pure cream.

thickened a whipping cream that contains a thickener (minimum fat content of 35%).

cucumber, lebanese short, slender and thin-skinned cucumber.

Has tender, edible skin, tiny, yielding seeds, and sweet, fresh and flavoursome taste.

daikon giant white radish; available fresh from Asian grocers.

pickled daikon pickled in rice bran and salt, is yellow, crunchy and very pungent. ·

dashi traditionally, three types of dashi are used in Japanese cooking: katsuo-dashi, stock from dried bonito flakes; konbu-dashi, stock from dried kelp seaweed; and niboshi-dashi, stock from dried sardines or anchovies. Instant dashi is available in powder, granules and liquid concentrate.

duck, chinese barbecued traditionally cooked in special ovens in China; dipped into and brushed during roasting with a sticky sweet coating made from soy sauce, sherry, ginger, five-spice, star anise and hoisin sauce. Available from Asian food shops as well as dedicated Chinese barbecued meat shops.

eggplant vegetable also called aubergine.

baby also called finger or japanese eggplant; very small and slender.

eggs if a recipe calls for raw or barely cooked eggs, exercise caution if there is a salmonella problem in your area, particularly in food eaten by children and pregnant women.

fish sauce called naam pla (Thai) or nuoc naam (Vietnamese); the two are almost identical. Made from pulverised salted fermented fish (most often anchovies); has a pungent smell and strong taste. Available in varying intensity, so use according to your taste.

flour

plain also known as all-purpose.

rice very fine, almost powdery, gluten-free flour; made from ground white rice. Used in baking, as a thickener, and in some Asian noodles and desserts.

self-raising plain or wholemeal flour with baking powder and salt added; make at home in the proportion of 1 cup flour to 2 teaspoons baking powder.

gelatine we use dried (powdered) gelatine; also available in sheets called leaf gelatine. Three teaspoons of dried gelatine (8g or one sachet) is roughly equivalent to four sheets.

ginger

fresh also called green or root ginger. Store, peeled, covered with dry sherry in a jar and refrigerated, or frozen in an airtight container.

pickled pink sweet pink pickled ginger eaten with sushi and sashimi

pickled red savoury red pickled ginger; sometimes used as a filling in sushi rolls.

gourd kampyo gourd or calabash pith; sold dry, in packets, or cooked and seasoned, in cans or refrigerated packets. Softened, it's used as a filling in rolled sushi or as a decorative tie around food.

hoisin sauce a thick, sweet and spicy chinese barbecue sauce made from salted fermented soybeans, onions and garlic. Available from Asian food shops and supermarkets.

japanese mint (shiso) also called perilla or beefsteak plant; a member of the mint family. Red shiso is less aromatic and used mainly to colour and spice pickles.

japanese parsley (mitsuba) use flat-leaf parsley if mitusba is hard to find.

kaffir lime leaves also called bai magrood; looks like two glossy dark green leaves joined end to end, forming an hourglass shape. Used fresh or dried, like bay leaves, in South-East Asian dishes. Sold fresh, dried and frozen, the

dried leaves are less potent so double the amount if using them as a substitute for fresh; a strip of fresh lime peel may be substituted for each kaffir lime leaf.

kalonji also called nigella seeds. Tiny, angular seeds, black on the outside and creamy within, with a sharp nutty flavour that is enhanced by frying briefly in a dry hot pan before use. Kalonji can be found in most Asian and Middle Eastern food shops. Often erroneously called black cumin seeds.

kecap manis a dark, thick sweet soy sauce used in most South-East Asian cuisines. Its sweetness is derived from either molasses or palm sugar.

kumara the Polynesian name of orange-fleshed sweet potato often confused with yam; good baked, boiled, mashed or fried similarly to other potatoes.

lemon grass also called takrai, serai or serah. A tall, clumping, lemon-smelling and tasting, sharp-edged aromatic tropical grass; the white part of the stem is used. Can be found, fresh, dried, powdered and frozen, in supermarkets, greengrocers and Asian food shops.

lotus root has a crisp texture and delicate flavour. It has small holes throughout its length, which, when sliced into rounds, looks like a flower. Fresh lotus root must be peeled and cooked before eating. Also available prepared and ready for cooking in cans, vacuum packs and frozen.

mayonnaise we use whole-egg mayonnaise unless stated otherwise.

mesclun pronounced mess-kluhn; also called mixed greens or spring salad mix. A commercial blend of assorted young lettuce and other green leaves, including baby spinach leaves, mizuna and curly endive.

milk we use full-cream homogenised milk unless stated otherwise.

evaporated unsweetened canned milk from which water has been extracted by evaporation. Evaporated skim or low-fat milk has 0.3 per cent fat content.

mirin a Japanese champagne-coloured cooking wine, made of glutinous rice and alcohol. It is used expressly for cooking and should not be confused with sake.

mizuna Japanese in origin; the frizzy green salad leaves have a delicate mustard flavour.

mushrooms

button small, cultivated white mushrooms with a mild flavour.

enoki tiny, pale, long-stemmed cultivated mushroom; grown and sold in clusters. They have a mild fruity flavour and slightly crisp texture.

oyster also known as abalone; grey-white mushrooms shaped like a fan. Prized for their smooth texture and subtle, oyster-like flavour.

shiitake *fresh*, are also called chinese black, forest or golden oak mushrooms. Although cultivated, they have the earthiness and taste of wild mushrooms. *dried* also called dried chinese mushrooms or donko; have a unique meaty flavour. Rehydrate before use.

shimeji also called beech mushrooms; cultivated mushrooms grown and sold in clumps. They are nutty-flavoured and slightly crunchy.

swiss brown also called roman or cremini. Light to dark brown in colour with full-bodied flavour.

mustard

japanese hot mustard available in ready-to-use paste in tubes or powder from Asian grocery stores.

wholegrain also called seeded. A French-style mustard made from crushed mustard seeds and dijon-style mustard.

nashi a true pear of Asian origin. It is sweet, juicy and crisp when ripe.

noodles

cellophane (harusame) are made from mung bean or potato starch.

fresh rice also called ho fun, khao pun, sen yau, pho or kway teow. Can be purchased in strands of various widths or large sheets of about 500g which are to be cut into the desired noodle size. Chewy and pure white, they do not need pre-cooking before use.

hokkien also called stir-fry noodles; fresh wheat noodles resembling thick, yellow-brown spaghetti needing no pre-cooking before use.

ramen popular Japanese wheat noodles, sold in dried, fresh, steamed and instant forms.

soba also known as buckwheat noodles, are made from differing proportions of buckwheat flour. Usually available dried, but can be purchased fresh from local noodle makers.

somen extremely thin noodles made from hard wheat – if eggless, they are labelled somen and tamago if made with egg. Traditionally eaten in cold dishes, can also be served in warm broth. Avoid overcooking, as they become gluggy.

udon thick, wide wheat noodles, available dried and fresh from most supermarkets and Asian food stores.

nutmeg a strong and pungent spice. Usually purchased ground, the flavour is more intense freshly grated from the whole nut (available from spice shops).

oil

olive made from ripened olives. Extra virgin and virgin are the first and second press, respectively, of the olives and are therefore considered the best.

sesame made from roasted, crushed, white sesame seeds; used as a flavouring rather than a cooking medium

vegetable any number of oils sourced from plant rather than animal fats.

onion

green also called scallion or (incorrectly) shallot; an immature onion picked before the bulb has formed, having a long, bright-green edible stalk.

spring crisp, narrow green-leafed tops and a round sweet white bulb larger than green onions.

pepper, japanese (shanso) ground spice from the pod of the prickly ash; related to sichuan pepper.

pickled plum puree (umeboshi puree) is made from plums (ume) slowly pickled in salt, with japanese mint (shiso) added for colour and flavour. It is available from health food stores or Asian grocers.

pork, chinese barbecued roasted pork fillet with a sweet, sticky coating. Available from Asian food shops or specialty stores.

potatoes

bintje oval, creamy skin, yellow flesh; good all-purpose potato, great baked and fried, good in salads.

kipfler small, finger-shaped, nutty flavour; good baked and in salads.

rhubarb actually a vegetable, rhubarb is a member of the buckwheat family. It has an intensely tart flavour which makes it a good dessert and pie filling when sweetened and combined with fruit.

rice, japanese (koshihikari) grown in Australia from Japanese seed; perfect for sushi. Found in supermarkets.

roasting/toasting spread nuts and dried coconut evenly on oven tray; roast in moderate oven about 5 minutes. Stir desiccated coconut, pine nuts and sesame seeds over low heat in heavy-based frying pan to toast more evenly.

rocket also called arugula, rugula and rucola; peppery green leaf eaten raw in salads or used in cooking. Baby rocket leaves are smaller and less peppery.

sake Japanese dry rice wine, sake, is a basic ingredient in many of the country's most well-known dishes. Special and first-grade sake is sold for drinking while ryoriyo sake, with its lower alcohol content, is made especially for use in marinades, cooking and dipping sauces.

sashimi fish sold as sashimi has to meet stringent guidelines regarding handling. Seek advice from local authorities before eating any raw seafood.

seafood

flying fish roe fine-grained, orange eggs of the flying fish; used as sushi filling and a topping for sushi.

japanese seafood sticks popular ingredient in sushi; buy the frozen Japanese product – it is of better quality and shreds more readily than Western-style seafood sticks.

prawns also called shrimp; available cooked or uncooked (green), with or without shells.

squid also called calamari; a type of mollusc. Buy squid hoods to make preparation and cooking faster.

seaweed

dried (wakame) a bright-green lobe-leafed seaweed usually sold in dry form and used in soups and salads. It shouldn't be simmered for more than a minute as it loses nutrients and colour. Dried wakame must be softened by soaking in water for about 10 minutes.

kelp (konbu) basis of dashi and simple boiled dishes to add slight flavour. Konbu should be thick and a glossy black or greenish brown in colour, and sometimes has a white powdery surface. Do not rinse but just wipe with a cloth or absorbent paper so as not to remove surface flavour; always remove konbu just before water boils because it can develop a bitter flavour if boiled. Cut the konbu pieces at intervals along edges to release extra flavour during the cooking process.

shredded (ao-nori) small pieces of shredded dried laver seaweed used as a garnish.

soft (nori) or dried laver; can be toasted quickly on one side over high heat or under preheated grill until it becomes slightly crisp.

toasted (yaki-nori) seaweed that is available already toasted in 10-sheet packets. Used in rolled sushi or crumbled over steamed rice with soy sauce. Can be refrigerated, frozen or stored in an airtight container and kept cool, dark and dry.

sesame seed paste is traditionally made by grinding toasted sesame seeds to a rough paste in a mortar and pestle, which is available ready made. Tahini (Greek-style sesame paste) is a reasonable substitute, however it is not made from toasted sesame seeds so there will be a difference in flavour.

sesame seeds black and white are the most common of this small oval seed, however there are also red and brown varieties. The seeds are used as an ingredient and as a condiment. Roast in a heavy-based frying pan over low heat.

seven-spice mix a Japanese blend of seven ground spices, seeds and seaweed. The mix varies but includes hot and aromatic flavours.

soy sauce made from fermented soybeans. Several variations are available in supermarkets and Asian food stores; we use japanese soy sauce unless indicated otherwise.

dark deep brown, almost black in colour; rich, with a thicker consistency than other types. Pungent but not particularly salty; good for marinating.

japanese an all-purpose low-sodium soy sauce made with more wheat content than its Chinese counterparts; fermented in barrels and aged. Possibly the best table soy and the one to choose if you only want one variety.

light fairly thin in consistency and, while paler than others, it is the saltiest. Not to be confused with salt-reduced or low-sodium soy sauces.

spinach also called english spinach and incorrectly, silver beet.

sugar

brown a soft, finely granulated sugar retaining molasses for its colour and flavour.

caster also called superfine or finely granulated table sugar.

palm also called nam tan pip, jaggery, jawa or gula melaka; made from the sap of the sugar palm tree. Light brown to black in colour and usually sold in rock-hard cakes; use brown sugar if unavailable.

tahini sesame seed paste; found in Middle Eastern food stores and the health food section of most supermarkets.

tamari similar to but thicker than japanese soy; very dark in colour with a distinctively mellow flavour.

tat soi also called pak choy and chinese flat cabbage; is a variety of buk choy. Its dark green leaves are cut into sections rather than separated and used in soups, braises and stir-fries. Available from some supermarkets and greengrocers.

teriyaki sauce traditional blend of soy sauce and mirin to brush over meat, poultry and seafood. Thick and thin varieties are available from supermarkets and Asian grocery stores.

tofu

firm made by compressing bean curd to remove most of the water. Good in stir-fries as it can be tossed without disintegrating.

deep-fried thin, deep-fried bean curd that can be opened to form a pouch; also available as seasoned bean curd

pouches in packets or cans. Atsu-age is a thicker version of deep-fried bean curd.

silken not a type of tofu but reference to the manufacturing process of straining soybean liquid through silk; this denotes best quality.

vanilla

bean dried, long, thin pod; the minuscule black seeds inside are used to impart a vanilla flavour in baking and desserts.

extract obtained from vanilla beans infused in water; a non-alcoholic version of essence.

vinegar

cider made from fermented apples.

rice a colourless vinegar made from fermented rice, flavoured with sugar and salt. Also called seasoned rice vinegar; sherry can be substituted.

sushi special blend of rice vinegar, sugar and salt used to make sushi rice. Ready-to-use sushi vinegar is available in liquid or powdered form.

wasabi japanese horseradish. Available in powder and paste form.

wombok also called chinese cabbage or napa cabbage; elongated in shape with pale green, crinkly leaves. Can be shredded or chopped and eaten raw

or braised, steamed or stir-fried.

worcestershire, japanese there are two types available, one similar to regular worcestershire and the other somewhat blander; both are made from varying proportions of vinegar, tomatoes, onions, carrots, garlic and spices.

wrappers wonton wrappers and gow gee or spring roll pastry sheets, made of flour, egg and water, are found in the refrigerated or freezer section of Asian food shops and many supermarkets. They come in different thicknesses and shapes: thin wrappers work best in soups; thicker ones are best for frying. The choice of round or square, small or large is dependent on the recipe.

gyoza thin pastry rounds made from wheat flour; used to wrap around fillings for Japanese dumplings and pot stickers. If unavailable, use gow gee wrappers.

yeast (dried and fresh), a raising agent. Granular (7g sachets) and fresh compressed (20g blocks) yeast can usually be substituted for each other.

yogurt we use plain full-cream yogurt.

index

conversion chart

MEASURES

One Australian metric measuring cup holds approximately 250ml, one Australian metric tablespoon holds 20ml, one Australian metric teaspoon holds 5ml.

The difference between one country's measuring cups and another's is within a two- or three-teaspoon variance, and will not affect your cooking results.North America, New Zealand and the United Kingdom use a 15ml tablespoon.

All cup and spoon measurements are level. The most accurate way of measuring dry ingredients is to weigh them. When measuring liquids, use a clear glass or plastic jug with the metric markings.

We use large eggs with an average weight of 60g.

LIQUID MEASURES

METRIC	IMPERIAL
30ml	1 fluid oz
60ml	2 fluid oz
100ml	3 fluid oz
125ml	4 fluid oz
150ml	5 fluid oz (¼ pint/1 gill)
190ml	6 fluid oz
250ml	8 fluid oz
300ml	10 fluid oz (½ pint)
500ml	16 fluid oz
600ml	20 fluid oz (1 pint)
1000ml (1 litre)	1¾ pints

LENGTH MEASURES

METRIC	IMPERIAL
3mm	⅛in
6mm	¼in
1cm	½in
2cm	¾in
2.5cm	1in
5cm	2in
6cm	2½in
8cm	3in
10cm	4in
13cm	5in
15cm	6in
18cm	7in
20cm	8in
23cm	9in
25cm	10in
28cm	11in
30cm	12in (1ft)

DRY MEASURES

METRIC	IMPERIAL
15g	½oz
30g	1oz
60g	2oz
90g	3oz
125g	4oz (¼lb)
155g	5oz
185g	6oz
220g	7oz
250g	8oz (½lb)
280g	9oz
315g	10oz
345g	11oz
375g	12oz (¾lb)
410g	13oz
440g	14oz
470g	15oz
500g	16oz (1lb)
750g	24oz (1½lb)
1kg	32oz (2lb)

OVEN TEMPERATURES

The oven temperatures in this book are for conventional ovens;
if you have a fan-forced oven, decrease the temperature by 10-20 degrees.

	°C (CELSIUS)	°F (FAHRENHEIT)
Very slow	120	250
Slow	150	300
Moderately slow	160	325
Moderate	180	350
Moderately hot	200	400
Hot	220	425
Very hot	240	475

First published in 2010 by ACP Magazines Ltd,

a division of PBL Media Pty Limited

54 Park St, Sydney

GPO Box 4088, Sydney, NSW 2001.

phone (02) 9282 8618; fax (02) 9267 9438

acpbooks@acpmagazines.com.au; www.acpbooks.com.au

ACP BOOKS

General Manager - Christine Whiston

Editor-in-Chief - Susan Tomnay

Creative Director & Designer - Hieu Chi Nguyen

Food Director - Pamela Clark

Published and Distributed in the United Kingdom by Octopus Publishing Group

Endeavour House

189 Shaftesbury Avenue

London WC2H 8JY

United Kingdom

phone (+44)(0)207 632 5400; fax (+44)(0)207 632 5405

info@octopus-publishing.co.uk;

www.octopusbooks.co.uk

Printed by Toppan Printing Co., China

International foreign language rights, Brian Cearnes, ACP Books bcearnes@acpmagazines.com.au

A catalogue record for this book is available from the British Library.

ISBN 978-1-74245-021-6